LESSONS IN T

NUMBER &PLACE VALUE

IN PRIMARY SCHOOLS

LESSONS IN TEACHING
NUMBER & PLACE VALUE
IN PRIMARY SCHOOLS

KATH MORGAN AND STEPHANIE SUTER

Los Angeles | London | New Delhi
Singapore | Washington DC

Learning Matters
An imprint of SAGE Publications Ltd
1 Oliver's Yard
55 City Road
London EC1Y 1SP

SAGE Publications Inc.
2455 Teller Road
Thousand Oaks, California 91320

SAGE Publications India Pvt Ltd
B 1/I 1 Mohan Cooperative Industrial Area
Mathura Road
New Delhi 110 044

SAGE Publications Asia-Pacific Pte Ltd
3 Church Street
#10-04 Samsung Hub
Singapore 049483

Editor: Amy Thornton
Development editor: Geoff Barker
Production controller: Chris Marke
Project management: Swales & Willis Ltd, Exeter,
Devon
Marketing manager: Lorna Patkai
Cover design: Wendy Scott
Typeset by: C&M Digitals (P) Ltd, Chennai, India
Printed and bound in Great Britain by: Henry Ling
Limited at the Dorset Press, Dorchester, DT1 1HD

Library of Congress Control Number: 2014942714

British Library Cataloguing in Publication Data

A catalogue record for this book is available from
the British Library

ISBN: 978-1-4462-9525-0
ISBN: 978-1-4462-9526-7 (pbk)

At SAGE we take sustainability seriously. Most of our products are printed in the UK using FSC papers and boards.
When we print overseas we ensure sustainable papers are used as measured by the Egmont grading system.
We undertake an annual audit to monitor our sustainability.

Contents

The authors

Kath Morgan worked in various schools before taking on a role as cross-phase advisory teacher for mathematics in a local authority. She then worked as senior lecturer in primary mathematics for several years before joining the National Numeracy Strategy as a senior regional director. Kath remained with National Strategies until 2011 when she took on her current role as member of the primary team at the University of Worcester, where she teaches on undergraduate and postgraduate mathematics modules. During her career she has also contributed to national programmes such as MEP and IMPACT and produced a range of curriculum materials (including TV programmes, videos, teacher handbooks and classroom materials). Her current research interests include approaches to written division and children's understanding of fractions.

Stephanie Suter is a senior lecturer in primary mathematics at the University of Worcester where she teaches undergraduate and postgraduate trainees. Her career started as a primary teacher. She taught in a diverse range of primary and lower schools where she had responsibility for leading subjects such as mathematics and ICT. She then joined a local authority as a consultant and supported schools to develop their teaching of mathematics. Before commencing her career in higher education she worked as a primary mathematics senior advisor for the National Strategy. During her career Stephanie has developed a wide range of mathematics curriculum materials and guidance for schools including CPD programmes, guidance booklets, CDs and videos.

Acknowledgements

Every effort has been made to trace the copyright holders and to obtain their permission for the use of copyright material. The publisher and author will gladly receive any information enabling them to rectify any error or omission in subsequent editions.

The authors would like to thank their families and friends for their support:

For Kath – Ceri and Becky

For Stephanie – Lily and Jack

Introduction

This book is intended to support trainee primary teachers and those supporting trainee teachers by linking theory to its practical application in the classroom. It does not aim to explore all areas of mathematics but to focus on aspects of number and place value. Children need an in-depth understanding of our number system in order to access effectively other elements of the number curriculum, such as addition, subtraction, multiplication and division. It is therefore an area of mathematics that should remain a high focus throughout the primary curriculum.

The content of this is book is structured around the 'Number and place value' sections of the programmes of study within the current National Curriculum (DfE, 2013). The initial chapters provide background information about the overall aims of the National Curriculum as well as an overview of the key elements of the programmes of study for Year 1 to Year 6, related to number and place value. At the end of the book there is a glossary of terms used and a summary of some of the key models, images and resources that are commonly used to support children's understanding in this area of mathematics.

In order to provide practical examples of how number and place value can be taught within the primary classroom, Chapters 4–12 are based around example lessons. These are not intended to be exemplar lesson plans that can simply be picked up and used in their entirety but have been written to provide ideas that can be adapted and developed. Each class is individual and unique and it is therefore impossible to produce a 'one size fits all' plan. A key feature of this book is therefore the accompanying text before and after each lesson plan, as this is intended to inform some of the decisions that are made as part of the planning process. These features include:

- an introduction providing background knowledge about the area of mathematics within the lesson;

- links to the Teachers' Standards that form a significant element of the lesson;

- a commentary to highlight and explore some of the pedagogical approaches used;

- an overview of potential challenges associated with the lesson, including common errors and misconceptions the children may encounter;

- some possible suggestions of ways in which the lesson could be adapted;

- ideas of ways the learning might be developed in future lessons;

- key self-evaluation questions to support reflection on practice.

Reference

DfE (2013) *The National Curriculum in England Key Stages 1 and 2 Framework Document.* London: Department for Education.

Chapter 1

Teaching the National Curriculum for mathematics

Learning outcomes

This chapter will help you to:

- engage with some of the aims that underpin the National Curriculum for mathematics;
- recognise the importance of developing both teacher and pupil confidence in numeracy and mathematical skills;
- consider the importance of providing opportunities for children to develop conceptual understanding, use mathematical language and solve problems in mathematics.

Maintained schools in England are legally required to follow the statutory National Curriculum and its programmes of study that outline the skills and processes that should be taught. However, although this core knowledge is outlined, schools and teachers need to make important decisions about how this content is taught. Indeed, in the overall aims of the National Curriculum (DfE, 2013, p6) the point is made that teachers can *develop exciting and stimulating lessons to promote the development of pupils' knowledge, understanding and skills.*

Extensive literature has already been written about good mathematics teaching. It is therefore not the intention of this chapter to summarise the rich sources of research and literature that already exist. Instead this chapter will focus attention on some of the messages in the introductory sections of the National Curriculum. These sections can easily be missed as it is tempting to head straight for the programmes of study to look at the content that needs to be covered. However they contain some important messages that may influence your approach to teaching this content.

Confidence in numeracy and other mathematical skills

The National Curriculum, within the introductory paragraphs on 'numeracy and mathematics', states that *Confidence in numeracy and other mathematical skills is a precondition of success across the National Curriculum* (DfE, 2013, p9). This highlights one very important factor that teachers need to consider when teaching mathematics. Sir Peter Williams, in the *Independent Review of Mathematics Teaching in Early Years Settings and Primary Schools*, identifies how *The United Kingdom is still one of the few advanced nations where it is socially acceptable – fashionable, even – to profess an inability to cope with the subject* (2008, p4). You may very well have heard adults making statements such as, 'I was never any good at mathematics'; however, it is interesting to consider whether you also hear adults making similar statements about other subjects, such as, 'I was never any good at reading'. In order to break this cycle it is important that children gain confidence in the subject and as teachers we need to work hard to develop and instil this confidence. Haylock (2010) describes his experiences of working with trainee teachers who expressed anxiety about teaching the subject. He explored their attitudes and found that they can stem from feelings of helplessness, inadequacy and fear around the subject that often evolve from their own experiences of being a learner in the classroom. In order to instil confidence in the children, teachers therefore need to overcome their own anxieties and feelings so that these are not inadvertently passed on to the children they teach. Williams makes the important point that *Confidence and dexterity in the classroom are essential prerequisites for the successful teacher of mathematics and children are perhaps the most acutely sensitive barometer of any uncertainty on their part* (2008, p3).

One way for primary teachers to gain confidence and overcome any feelings of helplessness and fear is to develop their own understanding and knowledge of the subject. However it takes a particular kind of 'subject knowledge' to become a confident teacher of mathematics. It might be assumed that those with higher formal mathematics qualifications are best placed to teach mathematics. Askew et al. (1997), however, found that this was not necessarily the case and that it was not the teachers with higher formal mathematics qualifications who necessarily helped children to make the highest gains. Instead this research found that the most effective teachers were those who had three types of knowledge: a deep knowledge and understanding of the mathematics they were teaching, a good knowledge of the children they were teaching and a good knowledge of relevant teaching approaches they could employ. It can therefore be argued that good knowledge of the subject involves a detailed understanding of the ideas and concepts that are being taught. This involves skills such as the ability to break mathematics down into steps and stages the children can understand and relate to and to be aware of the errors and misconceptions that children can make. Good knowledge also requires a detailed knowledge of what the children already know, understand and can do and their next steps in learning. Finally good knowledge also requires good pedagogical knowledge so that a variety of teaching approaches can be employed to help the children to learn effectively and to become confident mathematicians so that they do not go on to form the next generation of adults who profess an inability to cope with the subject.

The next sections in this chapter will consider some aspects of pedagogical knowledge. The introductory paragraphs of the mathematics National Curriculum (DfE, 2013, p99) identify the importance of children gaining an enjoyment and curiosity about the subject and also state that:

> *The National Curriculum for mathematics aims to ensure that all pupils:*
>
> - *become fluent in the fundamentals of mathematics, including through varied and frequent practice with increasingly complex problems over time, so that pupils develop conceptual understanding and the ability to recall and apply knowledge rapidly and accurately;*
>
> - *reason mathematically by following a line of enquiry, conjecturing relationships and generalisations, and developing an argument, justification or proof using mathematical language;*
>
> - *can solve problems by applying their mathematics to a variety of routine and non-routine problems with increasing sophistication, including breaking down problems into a series of simpler steps and persevering in seeking solutions.*

There is not scope in this chapter to discuss all of these ideas in detail. Therefore just one aspect from each aim will be discussed: conceptual understanding, using mathematical language and solving problems.

Conceptual understanding

Haylock (2010) suggests that, in order to promote positive attitudes to mathematics, the subject needs to be explained – an approach that requires deep understanding of mathematics, good knowledge of the children and the use of effective teaching approaches. He outlines the importance of shifting perceptions away from the idea that the subject can be taught by following rules and recipes towards an approach where understanding is developed. Skemp (1976) explored these two different approaches in depth and named them instrumental and relational understanding. He identified 'instrumental understanding' as learning mathematics by memorising and following sets of rules but without having an understanding of the reasons why these rules work. For example, when you learnt mathematics at school you may have been given the rule for multiplying numbers by ten as 'add a zero' and may have then been given the opportunity to use this rule by completing some examples. However you might not have been given the opportunity to explore this rule, to understand why this rule might work and to find out whether it does work in every circumstance. In contrast, Skemp therefore also identifies 'relational understanding'. This differs in that it involves not only knowing what to do to solve some mathematics but also understanding why and how it works. When using this type of teaching approach a teacher might instead model to children multiplying by ten by demonstrating how all of the digits move one place to the left and then a zero is added to the empty column as a place holder. While both approaches can in some cases lead to the correct answer, the second approach helps to avoid part-learnt or half-forgotten rules and the creation of easily avoided misconceptions when the rule does not apply to all numbers (for example $2.5 \times 10 \neq 2.50$). It is therefore relational understanding that supports the development of conceptual understanding and as teachers we need to help children to understand how and why the mathematics they are exploring works. This is also recognised in *Understanding the Score* (2008), an Ofsted report that provides an analysis of inspections of mathematics teaching. This report identifies the dangers of fragmenting mathematics and discourages teachers from presenting children with sets of rules to memorise without them understanding the contexts in which these rules work.

Our beliefs about mathematics can clearly influence the way in which we teach the subject. Askew et al. (1997) identified three different sets of beliefs about the way mathematics is taught and their research found that, although teachers might at times hold a range of different beliefs, they generally have a disposition towards one particular approach. In their research they identified 'discovery teachers' as those who place more emphasis on learning than teaching and view mathematics as something that should be discovered by children. The 'transmission teachers' were those who placed more emphasis on teaching than learning and view mathematics as a set of rules and procedures children should learn and use. Finally the 'connectionist teachers' were those who had a clear focus on helping children to establish connections between different aspects of mathematics and different representations of mathematics. The research found that teachers who had a strong connectionist orientation were more likely to have classes that made greater gains than those with a strong transmission or discovery orientation. It is therefore useful to consider ways in which mathematics can be represented.

Haylock and Cockburn (2013) provide a useful model that can be used when teaching children to develop understanding and make connections between new and previous learning and ways of representing mathematics. Figure 1.1 shows the four types of experiences that can be integrated into number-based mathematics lessons. Real objects can be provided for the children to handle and manipulate in order to give them physical experience of the mathematics and pictures can be used to show children images of the mathematics and how it might be drawn (the models, images and practical resources section at the back of this book provides examples of real objects and images that can be used when teaching number and place value). Alongside this, mathematical language can be used to describe the concrete experiences and images and mathematical symbols can be used to show how we might record them. This model links back to the introductory section of the mathematics National Curriculum, where the interconnected nature of the subject is recognised and therefore children *need to be able to move fluently between representations of mathematical ideas* (DfE, 2013, p99).

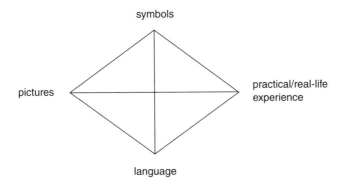

Figure 1.1 Important connections

Using mathematical language

Talk is a vital element of mathematics lessons and we need to encourage children from a young age to explain their thinking and justify their reasoning. This can be very difficult if they don't have the language in which to express themselves.

The National Curriculum acknowledges how *The quality and variety of language that pupils hear and speak are key factors in developing their mathematical vocabulary and presenting a mathematical justification, argument or proof* (DfE, 2013, p99). Therefore teachers need to actively support children in developing their use of increasingly precise mathematical language. Askew (2012) makes the useful distinction between *talking about mathematics* and *talking mathematics*. When children are learning a language such as Italian, we want them to talk Italian and not just talk about Italian. In the same way we need to engage children in the language of mathematics by talking mathematics rather than just talking about it. Enabling children to talk mathematics takes careful planning and consideration, particularly when children need to become familiar with a wide range of technical vocabulary that they are unlikely to use regularly and hear outside of the classroom in everyday conversation.

The *Mathematical Vocabulary* book (DfEE, 1999) provides guidance on ways in which you can plan opportunities to develop children's use of mathematical vocabulary. This includes providing the opportunity for children to listen to adults using words precisely and ensuring that children regularly have the opportunity to describe and compare the mathematics they are engaged with, to discuss how they are approaching and tackling the problems they have been set and to justify their methods, solutions and reasoning to others. Being able to express your thoughts in a logical and coherent way takes practice and an audience. The suggested lesson plans within this book suggest ways in which regular opportunities can be provided for children to engage in discussion in pairs, with the whole class and with the teacher. This provides children with opportunities to practise their explanations and to refine them from feedback and, importantly, helps teachers to gain an understanding of children's thinking and how this can be further developed. In order for meaningful discussion to take place children need something meaningful to talk about. To give children opportunities to develop an argument and have opportunities to explain and justify their thinking children need to be presented with problems to solve.

Solving problems

Problem solving should be a regular and integrated part of mathematics teaching and learning so that children have the opportunity to apply and reinforce the knowledge and skills they are learning. To identify when something actually poses a problem, Haylock (2010) identifies three Gs of problem solving: the given, the gap and the goal. A problem is only really a problem when some thinking is required in order to work out how to get from the given to the goal (or from the question posed to the answer provided). This highlights the importance of making sure children have experience of non-routine problems, as when tackling routine problems that have been encountered before, the gap between the given and goal may be obvious and so little problem solving might actually take place.

Problem solving can be narrowly interpreted as solving word problems. While children do need to develop the skills to solve word problems, problem solving is far wider and should be a more regular occurrence than this interpretation would suggest.

Problem solving should not be an activity that children only engage with at the end of a unit or sequence of lessons. Instead we need to engage children regularly with questions that pose a challenge to solve and require children to articulate and justify their thinking and demonstrate their level of conceptual understanding. For example, we could ask questions such as:

- How can we find out if 143 is a prime number?

- Davil says that if you add four even numbers, the answer is always even. How can we find out if he is right? Is his statement sometimes, always or never true? Why?

- I have covered up some numbers on this hundred square. How can we find out which ones they are? Convince me that you're right.

- If I know that 54 × 20 = 1080, what other calculations can you do easily? Why?

The Ofsted *Made to Measure* report was informed by visits to primary schools where there was good practice in teaching mathematics. One feature of good practice identified was that children were given extensive experience of problem solving and this *deepened their understanding and increased their fluency and sense of number* (Ofsted, 2012, p30). The report identifies how using and applying mathematics were integrated in effective schools into day-to-day teaching and how children were given problems in new or unusual contexts that required them to think hard and apply their knowledge. The teachers encouraged the children to discuss mathematical problems in depth and this helped to build their confidence and understanding (the ideas discussed in the previous sections). In one effective school, children were confident enough to 'think aloud' and were happy to share any mistakes they made so that they could be used to help others.

Good and satisfactory mathematics teaching

Table 1.1 (Ofsted, 2008, pp67–69) outlines some of the differences between good features and satisfactory features of mathematics teaching. Many of these elements relate directly to Chapter 3, on planning; however there are also features that relate to and reinforce the areas discussed above within this chapter. In good mathematics teaching children are given the opportunity to move beyond routine exercises in order to solve non-routine problems and open-ended tasks. The children expect to be given problems to solve and tackle these with independence. Good teachers of mathematics have good subject knowledge and use this to extend understanding and to help children make links and connections. Good teachers also encourage pupil discussion and children are expected to provide explanations of their reasoning.

Key self-evaluation questions to help reflection on practice

- Am I clear about the aims of the mathematics National Curriculum and decisions I need to make about how I might teach the content of the programmes of study?

- Do I feel confident teaching mathematics? If not, what do I need to do to gain confidence?

- Does my teaching focus on developing children's understanding of mathematics?

- Is talk a regular feature of my mathematics lessons? Do I provide opportunities for children to talk mathematics and to explain their thinking and reasoning?

- Do I regularly engage children in problem solving?

References

Askew, M. (2012) *Transforming Primary Mathematics*. London: Routledge.

Askew, M., Brown, M., Rhodes, V., Wiliam, D. and Johnson, D. (1997) *Effective Teachers of Numeracy*. London: Teacher Training Agency.

DfE (2013) *The National Curriculum in England Key Stages 1 and 2 Framework Document*. London: Department for Education.

DfEE (1999) *Mathematical Vocabulary*. Suffolk: DfEE Publications.

Table 1.1 Differences between good and satisfactory teaching of mathematics

	Features of good mathematics teaching (primary)	Features of satisfactory mathematics teaching (primary)
1	Lesson objectives involve understanding and make what is to be learned in the lesson very clear.	Lesson objectives are procedural, such as descriptions of work to be completed, or are general, such as broad topic areas.
2	Teaching features a successful focus on each pupil's learning. Pupils are clear about what they are expected to learn in the lesson and how to show evidence of this.	Teaching features a successful focus on teaching the content of the lesson. Pupils complete correct work and are aware of the lesson objectives but may not understand what they mean or what they need to do to meet them.
3	The lesson forms a clear part of a developmental sequence and pupils recognise links with earlier work, different parts of mathematics or contexts for its use.	The lesson stands alone adequately but links are superficial; for example, links are made with the previous lesson but not in a way that all the pupils understand.
4	Teachers introduce new terms and symbols meaningfully and expect and encourage correct use.	Teachers introduce new terms and symbols accurately and demonstrate correct spelling.
5	**Whole-class teaching/questioning** Pupils spend enough time listening to teachers' exposition and working to develop their understanding, and teachers move them on when appropriate. Teachers and support staff ensure all pupils participate actively in whole-class activity, such as through using mini-whiteboards or partner discussions. When offering answers or accounts, the teacher expects pupils to give explanations of their reasoning as well as their methods. Pupils are challenged if their explanations do not reflect their ability.	**Whole-class teaching/questioning** Teachers give effective exposition but pupils' understanding is limited due to time constraints or not extended due to limitations with the task. Questioning and whole-class activities are pitched appropriately but do not involve all pupils' actively; for example, few hands up, questions directed to few pupils, mini-whiteboards held up whenever pupils are ready so not all give answers or some copy from others. Questioning is clear and accurate but does not require explanation or reasoning; pupils describe the steps in their method accurately but do not explain why it works.
6	**Group/individual work** Teachers monitor all pupils' understanding throughout the lesson. They recognise quickly when pupils already understand the work or what their misconception might be. They extend thinking through building on pupils' contributions, questions and misconceptions to aid learning, flexibly adapting to meet needs and confidently departing from plans. The work challenges all pupils as it is informed by teachers' knowledge of pupils' learning; for example, through encouraging pupils capable of doing so to improve their explanations or use more efficient methods.	**Group/individual work** Competent questioning but the teacher may miss opportunities to respond to needs; for example, does not build on errors or sticks too closely to plans. Pupils generally complete work correctly but may have made errors or already understand the work so tasks do not fully stretch the high attainers or support the low attainers. Methods are clearly conveyed by teachers and used accurately by pupils; pupils focus on obtaining correct answers rather than enhancing understanding and questions may not be carefully selected. Skills may be short-lived so pupils cannot answer questions which they have completed correctly a few weeks earlier.

	Work requires thinking and reasoning and enables pupils to understand objectives fully. Pupils can explain why a method works and solve again a problem they have solved a few weeks earlier. Non-routine problems, open-ended tasks and investigations are used often by all pupils to develop the broader mathematical skills of problem solving, reasoning and generalising.	Typical lessons consist of routine exercises that develop skills and techniques adequately but pupils have few opportunities to develop reasoning, problem solving and investigatory skills, or only the higher attainers are given such opportunities.
7	Pupils develop independence and confidence by recognising when their solutions are correct and persevering to overcome difficulties because they expect to be able to solve problems; the teacher's interventions support them in estimating and checking for themselves.	Support generally offered to pupils does not develop independence in solving complete problems; for example, answers are given too readily or the problem is broken down so much that pupils do not know why the sequence of steps was chosen. Pupils may ask for help at each step and are given directed steps to take rather than interventions that encourage thinking and confidence that they can succeed.
8	Teaching assistants know the pupils well, are well briefed on the concepts and expected misconceptions and provide support throughout the lesson that enhances thinking and independence.	Teaching assistants facilitate access of all pupils, though may be less active in whole-class work.
9	Teachers (and pupils) have a good grasp of what has been learnt judged against criteria that they understand; this is shown through pupil discussion, reflection, oral or written summaries, and ascertained by the teacher's monitoring throughout the lesson.	Teachers (and pupils) make some accurate assessment of learning; for example, the teacher correctly reflects in a plenary what many pupils have achieved, pupils make an impressionistic assessment of their learning, such as using traffic lights or against a generic lesson objective.
10	Teachers' marking identifies errors and underlying misconceptions and helps pupils to overcome difficulties. For example, by setting clear targets, which pupils take responsibility for following up and seek to understand where they have gone wrong.	Accurate marking by the teacher identifies errors and provides pupils with feedback; important work has been marked by pupils or teacher.
11	Good use of subject knowledge to capitalise on opportunities to extend understanding, such as through links to other subjects, more complex situations or previously learned mathematics.	Any small slips or vagueness in use of subject knowledge do not prevent pupils from making progress.
12	Pupils exude enjoyment and involvement in the lesson. Pupils are confident enough to offer right and wrong comments. Pupils naturally listen to and respond to each other's comments, showing engagement with them.	Pupils enjoy making progress in an ordered environment. Some pupils offer responses to whole-class questions. Pupils listen to the teacher's and pupils' contributions and respond to them when asked to.

Haylock, D. (2010) *Mathematics Explained for Primary Teachers* (4th edn). London: Sage.

Haylock, D. and Cockburn, A. (2013) *Understanding Mathematics for Young Children*. London: SAGE.

Ofsted (2008) *Mathematics: Understanding the Score*. London: Ofsted.

Ofsted (2012) *Mathematics: Made to Measure*. London: Ofsted.

Skemp, R. (1976) Relational understanding and instrumental understanding. *Mathematics Teaching Journal*, 77, 20–26.

Williams, P. (2008) *Independent Review of Mathematics Teaching in Early Years Settings and Primary Schools*. Nottingham: DCSF Publications.

Chapter 2

Teaching number and place value

Learning outcomes

This chapter will help you to:

- identify the progression in number and place value through Key Stages 1 and 2;
- consider some of the ways in which children might develop a good understanding of number and the relationships between numbers;
- explore effective teaching and learning approaches to secure children's feel for and sense of number.

Children need to learn about numbers. They need to have what is commonly referred to as a sense of number, a feel for number (Anghileri, 2006) and a familiarity with numbers if they are going to work with them and handle them efficiently and effectively. Children need to understand the purpose of numbers and be comfortable with them if they are to be confident. Cockcroft (1982) used the phrase 'at-homeness' to suggest the familiarity we would like children to have with numbers.

Early counting

It is important for children to experience and become familiar with numbers used in different contexts: as a count of objects, actions or sounds, known as *cardinal* aspect; as a name (e.g. bus number, house number, class number, number on lottery ball), known as *nominal* aspect and in a positional context, known as *ordinal* aspect (i.e. first, second, third). Children learn to recite number names in order, initially starting with one, and this is often associated with a variety of 'counts'. For example, they may count steps taken whilst walking up the stairs or to the front door, they might count toys whilst setting them out and they could count children around their table. Some children can however recite number names without associating with any 'counts' and it needs to be remembered that, although knowing the number names in order is key to the counting process, there are also several other important components involved. In fact, there are five commonly accepted components associated with counting and these are identified by Gelman and Gallistel (1978) as 'how-to-count' principles. They are:

1. the one-to-one correspondence principle, which means that, when counting objects, just one number name is matched to just one object;

2. the stable-order principle, which means that the order of the number names when counting is always the same. One, two, three, four, five, is always the order for counting;

3. the cardinal principle, which means that the final number of the count is the number in the set of whatever is being counted;

4. the order irrelevance principle, which means that, when counting objects, it makes no difference in what order the objects are counted – the number in the set will always be the same;

5. the abstraction principle, which means that it makes no difference to what set is being counted, the above principles apply.

The variety of counting activities carried out in Early Years settings is often wide and relevant and planned for many different purposes. As teachers we need to ensure that this continues to be the case; sometimes counting activities can be restricted to counting pictures in a workbook with little relevance or meaning. Counting should have purpose. For example, how many children are at the art table? What does the notice say? How many apples are left after break? Will there be enough for everyone on green table to have one at lunch time? We are allowed four children on the mat: how many are on there now? How many children are away today? Some counting may be followed up with another question; at other times we may just simply want to know 'how many'?

As well as counting objects, children can count actions and sounds, both in mathematics and in other areas of learning. These opportunities need to be planned and made use of. Examples include jumping and counting actions in PE, listening to and counting coins being dropped into a container and the number of drum beats or hand claps.

National Curriculum 2013

The remainder of this chapter looks at the programmes of study for number and place value (DfE, 2013), considering some key ideas and ways in which we might work with children. Many are relevant throughout the primary phase and it is not intended that the sections are read in isolation from each other.

Throughout Key Stages 1 and 2 we want children to develop an understanding of number, extending the range of numbers they work with as they progress, building up their knowledge and awareness.

The National Curriculum for mathematics Key Stages 1 and 2 (DfE, 2013) provides stages of progression to consider.

Programmes of study Years 1 and 2

The introduction to the programmes of study for Key Stage 1 states:

> *The principal focus of mathematics teaching in Key Stage 1 is to ensure that pupils develop confidence and mental fluency with whole numbers, counting and place value . . .*
>
> *By the end of year 2, pupils should . . . be precise in using and understanding place value.*

For the Year 1 programmes of study, the section on number and place value includes the ability to:

- count to and across 100, forwards and backwards, beginning with zero or one, or from any given number;
- count, read and write numbers to 100 in numerals;
- count in multiples of twos, fives and tens;
- given a number, identify one more and one less;
- identify and represent numbers using objects and pictorial representations, including the number line, and use the language of: equal to, more than, less than (fewer), most, least;
- read and write numbers from 1 to 20 in numerals and words.

For the Year 2 programmes of study, the section on number and place value includes the ability to:

- count in steps of two, three and five from zero, and in tens from any number, forwards and backwards;
- recognise the place value of each digit in a two-digit number (tens, ones);
- identify, represent and estimate numbers using different representations, including the number line;
- compare and order numbers from zero up to 100;
- use <, > and = signs;
- read and write numbers to at least 100 in numerals and in words;
- use place value and number facts to solve problems.

Establishing the five key principles of counting, as previously described, is crucial before children can begin to learn what is set out above. Counting forwards and backwards can be done initially through singing and counting rhymes, some of which are learnt prior to Year 1. Rhymes can be accompanied by representations to illustrate the 'story'. So, for example, when singing 'Five Little Ducks', five ducks can be displayed and counted at the start and, as the song proceeds, the number of ducks is reduced, removing one duck at a time in line with the song. A number track can also be used so that, as the number of ducks decreases, the new number is shown/pointed to. These activities help children to make connections; they offer the numbers represented *practically* (ducks), as number *words* in the song and as *symbols* (numerals). Also, the process of decreasing the number of ducks and changing position on the number track can help to develop or consolidate children's understanding of the sequence of the counting numbers. The number words themselves could also be displayed as and when appropriate and children could use their fingers to show how many ducks remain at each part of the song. This network of connections, as mentioned in Chapter 1, is important for children to develop their concept of number (Haylock and Cockburn, 2008).

Although considerable attention is paid to counting backwards in number rhymes and songs using small numbers, this skill also needs to be considered when using larger numbers. Encouraging children to use different start and finish numbers can help them to gain familiarity with the range of numbers they are working with. For example, ask children to start with 7 and count on in ones until they get to 23 or start at 31 and count back in ones until they get to 9. These examples also include some of the boundary crossings children can find difficult and the teens numbers that can cause problems (see Chapter 5). Although it will be expected that children can eventually count without reference to supporting images, the use of number tracks, number lines and number squares can be powerful whilst children are developing this skill. Children can be asked to 'track the count' either on a large image for all children to see, or on individual images. Later counting activities would include counting forwards to go above 100 or counting back to go below 100, again boundaries that some children find challenging. Many number lines start at 0 and stop at 10, 20 or 100; however, when using numbers either side of 100, a 'partial' number line (e.g. a number line showing numbers from 80 to 120) might be helpful.

Part of number sense is being able to locate a number on a grid or number line, without having to count every number on the way. Knowing that 17 is between 10 and 20 on a number line or, later, knowing that 67 is between 60 and 70, and is in the sixties, is really helpful. For many children, this doesn't just happen and opportunities need to be provided where this can be learnt. Questions such as 'What do we know about 67?' or 'Where can I find 67 on the number line?' will help children to think about numbers in this way. It can be something we do not only with smaller numbers but also large numbers and later with decimal numbers, negative numbers and fractions.

Writing numbers is an important aspect of children's learning. In the early stages, children can develop their own marks to represent small numbers, often with remarkable appropriateness (Hughes, 1986). Children need to have some sense of numbers before we expect them to write the numerals. There seems little point in children beautifully scrolling the numeral 5 if they don't know how to read the numeral or if they are unable to count out five objects. Also, some children struggle to form numerals due to their slow development of fine motor skills. Although practising their numerals may help towards this development, it can be counterproductive to insist children over-practise their numeral formation. Recording their work can take a variety of forms: using number cards and marking a number on a number line or track can be appropriate ways of responding.

As children begin to record two-digit numbers, the slow emergence of the pattern in the way we say and write numbers needs to be explored and remembered. The difficulties with 'teens' numbers was referred to earlier but it is not in fact until the 70s that there is a consistent pattern in the way we say numbers. We use a rather interesting way of saying numbers in the teens, a 'back-to-front' system (seventeen for 17, saying the 7 first), but even when we reach the 20s we take on a slightly different word for what we might expect to be two-ty and this follows through until we reach seven-ty. Forty gets quite close, although we might expect it to be fourty, and so on. When teaching children how to write numbers we need to think carefully about how they are spoken. Chapter 5 also draws attention to another of the difficulties children may have when recording two-digit numbers. The chapter uses the example of twenty-five and describes how children may write this as 205 and provides ideas of images and representations to support children's learning. Place value cards in particular can be useful to help with this specific difficulty.

The programmes of study make reference to an understanding of place value. Chapter 5 provides useful ideas and background information associated with this 'big idea'. This chapter focuses on partitioning two-digit numbers into tens and ones. However, we would also like children to be thinking of a two-digit number in other ways. As indicated earlier, children should also know where to find the number on a number line or grid, know whether the number lies in a given interval, identify numbers smaller/bigger than it, know different ways of partitioning the number (e.g. know that 67 is also 50 and 17 or 40 and 27), know that 67 is 3 away from 70, know that it is 7 more than 60, know that it is 2 more than 65, and so on. The approach to different ways of partitioning a number is sometimes referred to as 'holistic' (Anghileri, 2006, p41); Anghileri also points out the advantage of using real examples to illustrate the importance of such an approach. For example, 67 pence is 50 pence and 17 pence more; 67 cm is 3 cm shorter than 70 cm. This knowledge does not come from simply being shown/asked for the place value of each digit or from reading and writing the numbers. It can be developed by the use of appropriate questioning and making use of a variety of models and images that help children see representations of numbers and where they are in relation to other numbers. The contextual approach also provides rich opportunities – for example, counting out money amounts.

Another aspect that is included in the programmes of study is counting in steps of different sizes – ones, twos, fives and tens in Key Stage 1. Children often find counting in twos quite easy, although they have to negotiate the peculiarity of the teens numbers early on. Various contexts can be used during the early stages, such as counting Wellington boots, feet, hands or socks. Seeing images of pairs of objects alongside the numbers representing the quantity helps children to see links between visual images, numerals and spoken words. Children generally count on in twos past 20 with relative ease and only seem to have difficulty if they already struggle with counting in ones. It can be important again to 'track the count'; it helps children to see where the numbers are and can avoid an unthinking recital of the words, especially if followed up with questions such as, 'Will 24 be in our count? How do you know? What about 57? Why/Why not? Can you give us a number between 50 and 60 that we would say if we carried on counting?' If using a hundred square, the numbers in the count could be marked or shaded and children could be asked what they notice. Can children predict other numbers? Children should be given the opportunity to start with different numbers and count backwards as well as forwards. For example:

- Start with 8 and count on in 2s until we get to a number bigger than 45. Let's mark the numbers we say.

- Now start with 22 and count on in 2s and cover up. What happens? Why?

- What if we start with 1 and count on in 2s – do you think we'll get some of the same numbers as before? Why/Why not?

- Start at 33 and count back in 2s. Which were tricky? Why?

There are lots of opportunities to engage children in thinking, predicting, explaining and making sense of number. The same sorts of activities can be used for children counting in fives and tens, although I did go into a Year 2 class once and when I asked if we could count in fives starting at 3, I was promptly told: 'No – if you want to count in fives, you have to start at five'. By the end of the lesson the children told me that I could start at any number and count in whatever I liked and counting in fives with different start numbers was like magic! Counting in fives, starting at different numbers, produces a pattern well worth exploring. It enables children to begin to 'get to know' numbers, suggest their own tasks and what might be described as 'take on ownership' of the numbers.

Being able to identify the number ten more than or less than a given number is a key skill in developing mental addition and subtraction but is not one that all children readily develop. Spending time counting on and back in tens from different starting numbers and linking this to images such as hundred squares, bead strings and number lines as the count carries on, as well as exploring and discussing the numbers in the count can be worthwhile. The types of questions as suggested earlier for counting up/down in twos could also be used. Varying the types of activities can give children the opportunity to work in different ways, with different images and for different reasons.

Counting in numbers of different sizes can help children to move towards establishing their multiplication tables and patterns noticed within and between the tables can be explored. There is a lesson plan in Chapter 7, which includes some ideas about how patterns might be used.

Years 3 and 4

The introduction to the programmes of study for lower Key Stage 2 (Years 3 and 4) includes:

> *The principal focus of mathematics teaching in lower Key Stage 2 is to ensure that pupils become increasingly fluent with whole numbers . . . including . . . the concept of place value.*

For the Year 3 programmes of study, the section on number and place value includes the ability to:

- count from 0 in multiples of 4, 8, 50 and 100; find 10 more or 100 more or less than a given number;
- recognise the place value of each digit in a three-digit number (hundreds, tens, ones);
- compare and order numbers up to 1 000;
- identify, represent and estimate numbers using different representations;
- read and write numbers up to 1 000 in numerals and words;
- solve number problems and practical problems involving these ideas.

For the Year 4 programmes of study, the section on number and place value includes the ability to:

- count in multiples of 6, 7, 9, 25 and 100;
- find 100 more or less than a given number;
- count backwards through zero to include negative numbers;
- recognise the place value of each digit in a four-digit number (thousands, hundreds, tens and ones);
- order and compare numbers beyond 1 000;
- identify, represent and estimate numbers using different representations;
- round any number to the nearest 10, 100 or 1 000;
- solve number and practical problems that involve all of the above and with increasingly large positive numbers;
- read Roman numerals to 100 (I to C) and know that, over time, the numeral system changed to include the concept of zero and place value.

Moving on to three-digit numbers is not just working with 'an extra digit'. Two-digit numbers such as thirty (30) and forty (40) have an obvious place for the zero, whereas numbers such as six hundred and eight (608) or three hundred and twenty (320) can be more challenging for some children to write down in numeral form. This has been alluded to earlier in the chapter but careful consideration needs to be made when we are expecting children to read, write, compare and order these numbers. Place value charts are referred to and illustrated in Chapters 5 and 10 (and can be powerful images to work with). They enable children to see how components of numbers can be combined and how multi-digit numbers might be partitioned. Place value cards can also be useful in considering digit values of a number. Whatever resources are used, they only form part of the support for learning; the language alongside is extremely important and the children should be using it. For example, if using the place value chart, children should be saying sentences such as, 'ninety thousand and forty five needs three numbers from the chart – ninety thousand, forty and five', ideally with the child making an indication on the chart as to where these numbers are.

As with two-digit numbers, children will need to realise that larger numbers can be partitioned in different ways. For example, 6437 can be partitioned into six thousand, four hundred, thirty and seven or it could be partitioned into sixty four hundreds, thirty and seven or six hundred and forty three tens and seven, and so on. It is when children are working with these numbers as part of calculations that they can make decisions about how to partition them to make them easier to work with. If they don't know they can partition them in different ways or don't know how to, they are limited in their approaches to the calculations.

At each stage of progression it is important that children's existing understanding is built on. If children's understanding and confidence with three-digit numbers are not secure, then there is little point in moving on to working with four-digit numbers. However, sometimes 'special' numbers can be explored (e.g. 4000); children might know what this number is and be able to count in thousands starting with zero, although unable to count in 50s starting with 450. Progression is not always tidy and there will frequently be large numbers that children can recognise and work with to some extent without having full understanding of other numbers of the same magnitude.

At all stages of children's learning, appropriate number lines can be used so that children gain some feel for the relative size and position of numbers. Children can suggest where numbers might be placed and provide a reason for their decision. As described when considering two-digit numbers, children should develop an 'awareness' of these numbers in the holistic sense.

Chapter 8 provides a lesson introducing negative numbers to Year 4 children. The idea of counting back, crossing zero and being introduced to negative numbers is often met with little difficulty, although realising that −4 is bigger then −6, for example, can initially cause problems. The chapter stresses the need for children to speak the numbers and make use of models, images and contexts for the learning. Having a sense of negative numbers may not conjure up the same feel as for positive numbers; we cannot imagine negative three shoes, for example, but we can make sense of negative three on a number line and what it means in contexts such as temperature or a lift that travels below ground.

Rounding numbers requires children to consider the degree of accuracy asked for and then to make a judgement based on their knowledge of the number being rounded. In the early stages, use of an appropriately marked number line can help children see what they are doing. So, for example, if children were rounding a set of numbers to the nearest 100, initially using a number line marked in 50s could assist.

We should try to avoid tasks which are always 'straightforward'; this does not challenge children in their thinking. So in 'rounding any number to the nearest 10, 100 or 1 000' we might ask

Round the following numbers to the nearest 100:

567   967   43

The first one is straightforward; it rounds up to 600. The second one rounds up to 1 000, although some children will think that cannot be right because they have taken the number up to 1 000, not realising that this is the nearest hundred, ten hundred. The last one is rounded to 0 or 0 hundred as that is the closest hundred to 43. They are all worth discussion but questions like these sometimes don't get asked because of fear the children will get confused. We must remember too, that rounding is often done for a purpose, not just for its own sake. Yes, children need to develop rounding skills but they must have the opportunity to make good use of them.

The Year 4 programmes of study also include a section 'number-fractions (including decimals)'. The accompanying notes and guidance (non-statutory) indicate that:

> children's understanding of the number system and decimal place value is extended at this stage to tenths and hundredths. This includes relating the decimal notation to division of whole number by 10 and later 100.

It is often thought that if children understand place value for whole numbers and understand ideas associated with the fractions tenths, hundredths and so on, then extending to decimal place value shouldn't be a problem. The ideas underpinning decimals are the same as those underpinning fractions (Hansen, 2011). It does mean, however, that if children don't have an understanding of fractions, they may struggle to develop a sense of and feel for decimals.

Many years ago, I was introduced to a model for place value with whole numbers that extended very neatly into decimal numbers. It was set within a bakery and the bakery vans.

- A slice of bread was regarded as a unit/whole/one: 1s.

- Slices were packed in tens – this was a loaf (10 slices/ones): 10s.

- Loaves were loaded on to shelves. Each shelf held ten loaves (100 ones): 100s.

- Ten shelves could be fitted into one van (1 000 slices): 1 000s.

- And there were probably ten vans in the fleet! (10 000): 10 000s.

This model was presented to children as a way of supporting their learning of whole numbers and place value. Later, when they were beginning to learn about decimals the model continued:

- Each slice of bread was cut into 'soldiers' (tenths): $\dfrac{1}{10s}$

- Each soldier was cut into croutons (hundredths): $\dfrac{1}{100s}$

This may not be the model for everyone but it extends well to decimals and provides an image of the relationships between the ones, tenths, hundredths, etc.

Whatever model is used to introduce decimals, care must be taken that if you are using a resource that has been used to represent different values within the base ten number system at an earlier stage, this needs to be acknowledged and brought to children's attention.

Years 5 and 6

The introduction to the programmes of study for upper Key Stage 2 (Years 5 and 6) includes:

> *The principal focus of mathematics teaching in upper Key Stage 2 is to ensure that pupils extend their understanding of the number system and place value to include larger integers.*

For Year 5, the the section on number and place value in the programmes of study includes the ability to:

- read, write, order and compare numbers to at least 1 000 000 and determine the value of each digit;

- count forwards or backwards in steps of powers of 10 for any given number up to 1 000 000;

- interpret negative numbers in context; count forwards and backwards with positive and negative whole numbers, including through zero;

- round any number up to 1 000 000 to the nearest 10, 100, 1000, 10 000 and 100 000;

- solve problems and practical problems that involve all of the above;

- read Roman numerals to 1 000 (M) and recognise years written in Roman numerals.

For Year 6 the section on number and place value in the programmes of study includes the ability to:

- read, write, order and compare numbers up to 10 000 000 and determine the value of each digit;

- round any whole number to a required degree of accuracy;

- use negative numbers in context, and calculate intervals across zero;

- solve number and practical problems that involve all of the above.

Both counting and using number lines should be part of children's mathematical 'diet' throughout Key Stages 1 and 2. Earlier in the chapter, counting using rhymes and song was discussed and then counting in steps of different sizes was referred to, with examples of questions that aimed to encourage children to think about the numbers that might be encountered. Counting can continue to be beneficial – counting forwards or backwards in 0.5s starting at 10.3 is very different to counting forwards in 1s starting from 0, for example. Counting forward in 200s starting with 145 can be quite challenging, as can counting backwards in 3s starting with 11 and crossing zero. At whatever stage children are in their learning, there are always counting activities that are appropriate and challenging.

In the early stages, using a number line marked and numbered in ones, with sometimes larger markings for 5, 10, 15, etc. or for 10, 20, 30, etc. can offer images to support children's awareness of 'where numbers sit' in relation to each other and their awareness of the sequence of numbers. As children progress, the range of numbers used on lines can change, as can the markings and numbering. In later Key Stage 2, a number line marked in 1000s can be used for children to give an approximate positioning for numbers such as 750 or 2356 and so on, particularly if they have the chance to think about and provide a reason for their choice. Within the context of number and place value, number lines showing negative numbers and decimals can also be used for counting and positioning.

Counting sticks can also be used as a resource to stimulate children's mental imagery. These are often sticks marked in ten sections but without numbers.

The 'start' and 'finish' (i.e. the two ends of the stick) numbers can be changed according to the level of challenge required. Indicating a start of 0 and a finish of 10 and asking children to count up or down the number line, as each mark is pointed to in order, then pointing to 'random' marks along the line and asking for the numbers to be given, is one of the easier tasks. Indicating a start of 5 and a finish of 5.1 (see Figure 2.1) with similar activities as above is several stages further on. Again, a counting stick can be used throughout the Key Stages and appropriate challenges can be matched to the stage of children's learning and the types of numbers they are working with.

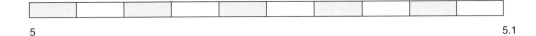

5   5.1

Figure 2.1 Using a counting stick

Chapter 10 provides a lesson suggestion for Year 5, focusing on 'big numbers'. It also identifies some of the aspects that children might struggle with. Reading out loud and writing large numbers are not straightforward and the point was made earlier that children need to develop their understanding of multi-digit numbers through similar activities and experiences as those used for two-digit numbers, using extended models and images if they are to 'make and keep friends' with the numbers they meet. 'Speaking numbers' is crucial and links between the spoken form, written form (numeral and words), models and images continue to help children make the connections that are so important.

Our aim is for children to be able to handle numbers confidently and efficiently, not just when reading, writing and ordering numbers but to allow numbers to (what I term) 'talk to them' when working with them; in other words, look at the numbers and 'listen to'/look out for what they are telling you about themselves. You can use what you can see/know about them (or hear from them!) to help you carry out your work with numbers. Children can gain this level of familiarity by having experience of appropriate models and images, by talking numbers and by being asked questions which prompt them to look out for what is in the numbers.

Key self-evaluation questions to help reflection on practice

- Am I aware of the stage of learning my children are at and do I know what they might move to next?

- Do I look out for errors and misconceptions and do I know how these might be addressed/minimised?

- Do I use a range of representations of number and encourage children to use and talk about them?

- Am I aware of how a feel for number will impact on their confidence with calculating?

References

Anghileri, J. (2006) *Teaching Number Sense*. London: Continuum.

Cockcroft, W. (1982) *Mathematics Counts: Report of the Committee of Inquiry into the Teaching of Mathematics in Schools*. London: HMSO.

DfE (2013) *The National Curriculum in England Key Stages 1 and 2 Framework Document*. London: Department for Education.

Gelman, R. and Gallistel, C.R. (1978) *The Child's Understanding of Number*. Cambridge, MA: Harvard.

Hansen, A. (ed.) (2011) *Children's Errors in Mathematics* (2nd edn). London: SAGE.

Haylock, D. and Cockburn, A. (2008) *Understanding Mathematics for Young Children*. London: SAGE.

Hughes, M. (1986) *Children and Number*. Oxford: Blackwell.

Chapter 3

Planning: telling the 'story' of the lesson

Learning outcomes

This chapter will help you to:

- recognise the importance of identifying focused objectives and success criteria that can be achieved within a lesson;
- ensure that your planning provides a clear indication of what the adults and the children are doing throughout the lesson;
- develop your ability to identify and use key questions in your planning.

Planning is an important part of teaching, and developing planning skills is a key aspect of learning to become a good teacher and a good teacher of mathematics. In the early stages of teaching, writing detailed lesson plans can feel like a lengthy and time-consuming process. However the process involved in writing a lesson plan encourages you to focus not only on the important features of an effective lesson but also to tell the story of how the lesson will unfold and the strategies that will be used to help the children to learn.

Planning becomes easier with experience. It develops as your knowledge of the children, their prior learning and their individual needs grows, as your subject knowledge and awareness of difficulties children may encounter develop and as you become aware of a wide range of pedagogical approaches that can be employed. However in the early stages of learning to plan there are some frequently encountered areas of development for trainee teachers. These include having a clear focus for the lesson, planning for both the teacher and the children and making use of effective questioning. These three areas are therefore the focus for the first section of this chapter. In the second section an example planning grid provides an overview of key sections to consider when planning. The final section provides some key self-evaluation questions to support reflection on current practice and identify potential areas of development.

Focused objectives

In the majority of primary schools, children have a daily mathematics lesson. As there are approximately 38 weeks in a school year then children could have up to 190 mathematics lessons each year. This is worth mentioning because one of the common issues in the early stages of planning is trying to cover too much in each lesson. The objectives we use to plan from typically outline what we hope most children will achieve by the end of the academic year. They are therefore generally too large and there are too many elements of the objective to cover in just one lesson. Consider, for example, the following statement from the Year 1 programme of study from the National Curriculum (DfE, 2013, p102) *count to and across 100, forwards and backwards, beginning with 0 or 1, or from any given number*. There are many different elements to this statement, for example:

- Counting to 100 can be a complex process for Year 1 children who will need to learn the counting names to 20 with very little pattern to help them and then learn how to count over each decade (e.g. 27, 28, 29 ...). They then need to apply this to count across and beyond 100.

- In addition to counting forwards children need to be able to count backwards – something they often find harder because they have less experience of it.

- They also need to be able to count forwards and backwards starting with any number. Again, if they have only had experience of counting from 0 or 1 and little experience of counting backwards they will initially find this challenging.

In each lesson we therefore need to be clear about what we want children to learn and achieve. This helps us to be clear about what we are teaching and exactly what we will be looking for in order to know if children have reached our focused objective/s.

In addition to having a clear and precise focus for a lesson you need to be mindful of any connections you may want to make between other objectives and aspects of learning. The National Curriculum programmes of study have been organised into discrete areas of mathematics to help schools. However the National Curriculum also clearly states that we want children to *make rich connections across mathematical ideas to develop fluency, mathematical reasoning and competence in solving increasingly sophisticated problems. They should also apply their mathematical knowledge to science and other subjects* (DfE, 2013, p99). Your lesson may therefore focus on elements of more than one objective. In the examples above you may want the children to read as well as recite the numbers, even though this is mentioned in a different statement in the programmes of study. You can also look for opportunities to reinforce this understanding outside of the mathematics lesson, either in other curriculum areas or during other times of the school day (for example, as children are getting ready to go to assembly or go out for lunch).

Adults and children

In any lesson there are two very important sets of people to plan for: the adults and the children. The children are obviously the key consideration of the lesson. Their prior learning needs to be taken into account, as do the different needs and abilities within the class. A clear idea of how to simplify and extend the mathematics is therefore important in order to provide effective differentiation. This is important not only to cater for different ability groups but also when a plan B is needed! There are times when children may find an aspect of mathematics more challenging than we expected. At times such as these we need to think on our feet and adapt the lesson. There are other times when children complete a task much more quickly than expected or are not being challenged by the task set. In situations such as these extension activities help us to move the children on in their learning. The children also have a role to play not only in individual and group work but also during whole-class sessions. Planning should therefore take into consideration how they will interact during these periods of teaching. The use of individual whiteboards and pens is one approach that encourages all children to interact and respond to questions (as opposed to a hands-up approach, when only one child might get the opportunity to answer).

A good lesson plan not only outlines the mathematics and activities that different groups of children will be engaged in but also outlines what the teacher (and, when appropriate, any additional adults or support staff) will be doing throughout the lesson to teach the children and to help them learn. In lesson plans the teaching that will take place should therefore be explicit. During the teaching input this might include how the mathematics will be explained, what might be modelled or demonstrated to the children, questions that will be asked to help assess the children's understanding, language and vocabulary that will be highlighted and used. While the children are working planning may indicate any groups of children the teacher and/or support staff may work with intensively to provide additional input.

Questions

Questions are a crucial part of mathematics teaching and learning and therefore some key questions should be identified when planning a lesson. It can be easy to ask children the same kinds of questions, particularly those that are closed and only require children to recall a fact or give a one-word answer. However it is more open questions that can require children to think more deeply and give sustained answers, therefore helping adults to begin to assess the depth of their understanding and identify any potential misconceptions. Consequently, although it is important to ask a range of questions, whilst planning it is useful to identify a few good questions you can ask during a lesson that will encourage children to think, to explain their thinking and therefore give more detailed answers. When you identify a closed question that you could ask, such as, 'What does the digit 2 stand for in each of these numbers – 25 and 52?', think about whether you could rephrase the question so that it demands a higher level of thinking. Using words such as how and why can often help. This would change the question to, 'How do you know what the digit 2 stands for in each of these numbers – 25 and 52?' or 'Why does the digit 2 stand for different amounts in the numbers 25 and 52?'

There are different sources of types of questions you can use in your teaching. The *Mathematical Vocabulary* book provides useful examples of different types of questions along with examples of how to make closed questions into more open questions that will promote greater thinking and dialogue (DfEE, 1999, pp4–5). Bloom's taxonomy (1956) is also used in schools as it provides a hierarchy of different types of questions that can be used to help develop a focus on higher-order thinking.

Finally the booklet *Using Assessment to Raise Achievement in Mathematics* (QCA, 2003, p9) provides the following set of useful questions that can be adapted in order to ask questions that will provide you with useful assessment information:

- How can we be sure that . . . ?

- What is the same and what is different about . . . ?

- Is it ever/always true/false that . . . ?

- Why do _, _, _ all give the same answer?

- How do you . . . ?

- How would you explain . . . ?

- What does that tell us about . . . ?

- What is wrong with . . . ?

- Why is _ true?

Lesson plans

There are many different lesson-planning proformas and the format of these and the headings used will vary from school to school. The format within this book uses the idea that a lesson will have a beginning, middle and end and therefore has a section for each of these three elements. The other sections are those that are frequently seen on planning formats and are key elements to help think through the story of the lesson. Many plans also outline the context of the lesson and the prior learning of the class. The lesson plans in this book serve as example plans and therefore don't include this information.

Below are some prompts suggesting what might be recorded in each section of the planning format.

Year group	
Focused learning objectives	**Success criteria**
List here the objectives for the lesson. Try to make them as clear and precise as possible and don't be tempted to write too many. Depending on the lesson, you may have a different objective for the starter/introduction than you do for the main part of the lesson.	In order to develop your success criteria, try to analyse the route to meeting the objectives. What will you be looking out for as children progress? What skills, knowledge and understanding will children need to have in order to meet the objectives? What will the children do or say that will help you know they are meeting your objective?
Vocabulary	
List here the vocabulary you want the children to learn and use during the lesson. There is no need to list all mathematical vocabulary, but include the words/phrases that might be new or that children may need reminding of.	
Resources	
List here the resources you and/or the children will be using during the lesson. To help organise these resources, you might find it helpful to list separately what will be needed during the starter/introduction, the main part of the lesson and the plenary.	
Possible errors, misunderstandings and misconceptions to look out for	
Indicate here any anticipated mathematical errors and misconceptions as well as any misunderstandings associated with tasks set. This will prompt you to look out for any of these during the lesson.	

Timing	Starter/introduction
Indicate the timings for each part of the lesson – this helps you to judge what you can realistically do within one lesson.	This part of the lesson is sometimes used to provide an introduction to or preparation for the main part of the lesson and at other times is used as a rehearsal/reminder of mathematics children have not experienced for a while. Describe carefully what you will do and say and what you will ask children to do. List some of the key points to be made and key questions to be asked. Think about and explain how you will engage all children in this part of the lesson (e.g. will the children use individual whiteboards and pens? will the children have the opportunity to share ideas with a talk partner?) *Support* Include here ways in which some children can be supported in this part of the lesson. These may include: <ul><li>targeted questions aimed at particular individuals/groups of children;</li><li>prompting questions that provide extra scaffolding;</li><li>additional language alongside that being used in the lesson to help children make sense of the ideas and/or questions being explored;</li><li>additional resources to support thinking;</li><li>input/support from an additional adult or another child.</li></ul> *Challenge* Include here ways in which some children can be further challenged in this part of the lesson. These may include: <ul><li>extending the task;</li><li>probing questions to challenge thinking further;</li><li>input from an additional adult.</li></ul>
Timing Incorporate timings as appropriate for different stages.	**Main** Describe carefully what you will do and say and what you will ask children to do. Provide a level of detail that would inform an observer of what to expect to see happening during the lesson and to know who was doing what, how it was being organised and what the intended outcomes were – both in learning and in completion of tasks. Make links to prior learning and aim to build on this. Try to make sure there is a balance between whole-class teaching and focused teaching with groups or individuals. At all stages,

	make clear what you will be doing, what the children will be doing and what any additional adults will be doing.
	Signal clearly the change in stage/activity/focus during the lesson and indicate how this will be managed.
	Indicate who your questions will be targeted at (whole class, pairs, individuals, etc.) and how feedback is to be taken, including the main points you want to draw from feedback.
	Include actual key questions, including those used for assessment.
	Support and challenge
	Think about how you might offer different levels of support and challenge to the activities:
	• You might differentiate the task by setting different tasks for different abilities.
	• You might differentiate by offering additional modelling/ adult support to specific groups of children.
	• You might set an open-ended task that allows children to respond at different levels.
	• You might provide different resources to different groups of children.
	Be prepared to offer support for children from any ability group who find the task challenging and to challenge any children whose learning needs extending.
Timing	**Plenary/conclusion**
Try and plan your timings so you have time to include a plenary.	This part of the lesson can be used for a variety of purposes. It should not be used for a 'show and tell'-type activity and should be seen as a key part of the lesson and still part of the learning time.
	Describe clearly what you will do and what you will ask children to do. List any key questions.
	Think about how you might:
	• address any errors or misconceptions;
	• gather information to inform the next lesson (your own assessment as well as children's self-assessment);
	• draw together what has been learned and summarise key ideas to be remembered;
	• continue the learning;
	• involve all children.

Assessment opportunities

List here some of the key questions you will want to ask children as they are working.

It can be challenging to assess all of the children all of the time throughout all of the lesson. You might want to focus on those children whose level of understanding you are unsure about. These might be children you think are unclear or children whose thinking you can extend.

Key self-evaluation questions to help reflection on practice

Do your lesson plans:

- have focused objectives and success criteria that can be achieved within the lesson?

- include key questions that will help you to extend children's thinking and assess the depth of children's understanding?

- list the mathematical vocabulary to be introduced and used by children and adults?

- indicate any anticipated errors and misconceptions?

- provide a clear picture of what you (the teacher) will be doing throughout the lesson?

- provide a clear picture of what the children will be doing throughout the lesson?

- provide a clear indication of the role of any another additional adults throughout the lesson?

- clearly indicate how the work will be differentiated for different abilities?

References

Bloom, B. S. (1956) *Taxonomy of Educational Objectives*, vol. 1. Harlow: Longman.

DfE (2013) *Mathematics Programmes of Study: Key Stages 1 and 2.* London: Department for Education.

DfEE (1999) *Mathematical Vocabulary*. Suffolk: DfEE Publications.

QCA (2003) *Using Assessment to Raise Achievement in Mathematics*. Suffolk: QCA Publications.

Chapter 4

Year 1: One more than, one less than

Reference to the Teachers' Standards

Working through this chapter will help you meet the following standards:

2. Promote good progress and outcomes by pupils.
4. Plan and teach well-structured lessons.
5. Adapt teaching to respond to the strengths and needs of all pupils.
6. Make accurate and productive use of assessment.

Links to the National Curriculum (DfE, 2013)

Year 1 programme of study (statutory requirements)

Pupils should be taught to:

- given a number, identify one more and one less.

Introduction

Being able to identify one more than and one less than a given whole number is a crucial skill, and knowing that one more than a number is the next number and knowing that one less than a number is the previous number are things that children need to learn. Haylock and Cockburn (2008) identify these as basic principles of counting and stress the importance of making these principles explicit to the children.

We can help children to make links with addition and subtraction, using familiar practical contexts, describing 'the story' initially and then developing this into generalisations and further abstractions.

To support children you can make use of materials such as number tracks and number lines. Do take care when using these, as they do differ.

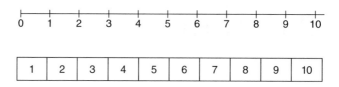

Figure 4.1 Number line and number track

Number tracks label a space and normally start at 1; number lines label a point on the line as a number and, at this stage, normally begin with 0, although the line is continuous. There are no 'gaps' between the numbers on a number track, whereas there are gaps between numbers on a number line. (Note: A 1–100 number grid is a number track rearranged – imagine a 1–100 number track, then cut up into strips of ten, then rearranged to form a square. This square arrangement can be very useful for children to see the patterns within the numbers 1–100.) Number lines also provide an important visual image which can help children make sense of the number system.

There is a focus on children speaking and listening in the lesson for this chapter; it is important that children use the language of 'one more than' and 'one less than' in relation to the numbers used and in relation to a model or image if they are going to make sense of and use these ideas. Generally, ideas associated with 'less than' are more difficult for children to grasp and the phrase itself is not readily used by children, so it is important for teachers to use this terminology and to provide opportunities for children to use it.

We must also be aware that, when referring to 'countables' (e.g. objects, sounds, actions), we should use the language 'fewer than' rather than 'less than'. It is sensible to refer to the number track when reinforcing the language of 'less than'. We can use the language 'one less than 9 is 8', for example, when using the number track because we are referring to the numbers themselves.

Children should have had frequent opportunities to count backwards and forwards in different contexts, and from different starting points, before moving towards these objectives. These might have included number stories, songs and rhymes. It is important that these have been associated with some representations of the numbers involved and connections made between the words being spoken/sung and these representations. This helps children understand that, as they count on, the quantity represented by the number becomes larger and, when counting back, becomes smaller.

The lesson has been set out so that there are two stages: the first stage is to introduce the idea of 'one more than' and the second one is to introduce the idea of 'one less than'. It has been organised in this way to separate these ideas initially and to provide clearer structure. They can be used flexibly; you may decide to carry out the two stages on different days if it suits the needs of your children better. Although these two ideas should ultimately be connected (see the section on how the learning might be developed in future lessons, below), they are not done so in this lesson.

Lesson plan

Year 1: One more than, one less than	
Focused learning objectives	**Success criteria**
Stage 1: To identify one more than, when counting objects	Count on in ones from a given number
	Identify one more than a given number on a number track
To identify one more than any given number up to 30	
	Use the language 'one more than' in a number sentence
Stage 2: To identify one less than, using a number track	
	Count back in ones from a given number
To identify one less than any given number up to 30	Identify one less than a given number on a number track
	Use the language 'one less than' in a number sentence

Vocabulary

one less than, one more than

Resources

Stage 1

- Bag or tin and some counters (a tin helps to create opportunity for the listening aspect to counting, so it is good to use counters that will make a noise as they are dropped into the tin)
- Number tracks to 30 (one large enough for all children to see and table-top versions, one between two children)
- Sets of number cards 0–29 (pairs of children need a selection within the range – so perhaps need five or six sets)
- Teddy counters (one teddy between two children)

Stage 2

- Bag or tin as used in stage 1
- Number tracks to 30 (one large enough for all children to see and table-top versions, one between two children)
- Sets of number cards 2–31 (pairs of children need a selection within the range – so perhaps need five or six sets)
- Teddy counters (one teddy between two children)

Plenary

- Set of number cards to show children (some numbers in range 0–30) and a bag to put them in
- Whiteboards and pens for children to use

Timing	Stage 1
10 minutes	Using a tin and some counters, ask children to watch and listen to you putting in counters. Drop in counters, one at a time, and ask the children to count out loud with you as you go along. Stop when you get to 8. Identify 8 on the number track. Show another counter and ask how many there would be in the tin if you were to put in one more counter. Ask children to talk to their partner and agree what it would be and how they know. Take feedback, acknowledging that it would be 9 and ask someone to identify this number on the number track. Put in the counter and 'tell the story', i.e. 'I put in 8 counters, then I put in one more, now there are 9. So, one more than 8 is 9'. Refer to the number track as you do so, emphasising the next number after 8 is 9 and connecting these ideas. Ask the children to talk to their partner and take it in turns to retell this story. Explain that you will be listening to their conversations and you may ask some to repeat their 'story' to the whole class.

Continue to drop counters into the tin, continuing to count on from where you stopped previously and repeat as above for other numbers, for example, 12 and 19, establishing that one more than 12 is 13 and one more than 19 is 20 (these are important thresholds for some children). Encourage children to 'tell the story' each time so that they are all using the number names and the language 'one more than'. You can repeat with other numbers if you wish.

Support

Provide number tracks for some pairs of children to assist their discussion.

Challenge

Children could be asked to 'tell stories' for numbers other than the one(s) you have provided. For example, 'I put in 29 counters, then I put in one more . . . . Can you say this in a sentence?' |
| 15 minutes | *Teddy moves – one more than*

Select two children and demonstrate the activity to everyone before asking all children to work in pairs.

Using some number cards in the range 0–29 (shuffled, and placed face down in a stack), children take it in turns to turn over a card. Using the number track they place the teddy counter on the number they have turned over. They then have to decide where teddy needs to be placed if he has to move on to the number which is one more than the number he is placed on at the moment. They have to tell the story for teddy. 'Teddy was put on 6, one more than 6 is 7, so he has to move to 7', moving |

	teddy as they do so. Children have to listen to each other and agree before they can change over roles. Each time, teddy will need to be taken off the track before the next turn. When all cards have been used, they can be turned over, shuffled and used again. *Support* Use number cards 0–10 and a number track from 0 to 11. *Challenge* Use a 1–100 number grid and a set of numbers cards reflecting this range. You only need to use a selection of the numbers; no need to have all cards 0–99.
10 minutes	**Stage 2** Show the children the tin with 9 counters inside. Recount what happened at the beginning of the lesson; you put 8 counters in, then another one, so there were 9 counters, because one more than 8 is 9 (point to number track). Now ask how many there will be if you now take out one counter. Ask children to talk to their partner and agree what it would be and how they know. Take feedback, acknowledging that it would be 8, and ask someone to identify this number on the number track. Using the number track, point out the number 9 and 'tell the story': 'We had 9 counters in the tin, we took out one so now there are 8 because one less than 9 is 8 and 8 is the number before 9', connecting these ideas. Point to the appropriate numbers on the number track as you are telling the story. Ask the children to talk to their partner and take it in turns to retell this story. Explain that you will be listening to their conversations and you may ask some to repeat their 'story' to the whole class. Select one or two children to retell the story. Repeat for other numbers used, each time referring to numbers on the number track.
15 minutes	*Teddy moves – one less than* Select two children and demonstrate the activity to everyone before asking all children to work in pairs. Using some number cards in the range 1–31 (shuffled, placed face down in a stack), children take it in turns to turn over a card. Using the number track they place the teddy counter on the number they have turned over. They then have to decide where teddy needs to be placed if he has to move on to the number which is one less than the number he is placed on at the moment. They have to tell the story for teddy. 'Teddy was put on 8, one less than 8 is 7, so he has to move to 7',

moving teddy as they do so. Children have to listen to each other and agree before they can change over roles. Each time, teddy will need to be taken off the track before the next turn. When all cards have been used, they can be turned over, shuffled and used again.

Listen in to conversations and identify two children who are using the correct language for their activity. Ask them to demonstrate to others what they are saying and praise the two children for carrying out the activity so well and using the correct language to tell the story.

Support

Use number cards 2–11 and a number track from 1 to 10.

Provide them with the phrase 'one less than' on a card that they can use when telling the story. Model the activity again before asking the children to work in pairs.

Challenge

Use a 1–100 number grid and a set of numbers cards reflecting this range. You only need to use a selection of the numbers; no need to have all cards 2–101.

Some children might be challenged to use numbers beyond this range. Make sure they can carry out the activity for numbers 1–100 without using the grid before this challenge is set.

Timing	Plenary/conclusion
10 minutes	Put the number cards in a bag. Invite a child to take one out and read it to the rest of the children. Ask children, 'On your boards, can you write down the number that is one more than . . .'. Allow a few seconds and then ask all to show their number. Now model giving the answer. 'One more than . . . is . . .'.
	Repeat this several times but now ask a different child to give the answer starting with the words, 'One more than . . . '.
	Now repeat as above, drawing numbers out of the bag but this time asking if children can write down the number which is one less than the number drawn from the bag, following it up with your modelling and then asking children to give the answer in a sentence, 'One less than . . . is . . .'.
	You may need alternative ways for some children to provide the number asked for (if they have difficulty writing the numbers). You could, for example, use a grid of numbers up to 30, and they can 'answer' by pointing to the numbers on the grid as they speak.

Assessment opportunities

Whilst they are working, ask children questions such as these. You might want to focus on those children whose level of understanding you are unsure about. These might be children you think are unclear or children whose thinking you can extend.

- Can you explain to me why teddy has been moved from 20 to 21?
- Suppose someone said that teddy now needs moving to 23. Would they be right?
- This teddy has just been moved to 17. What number has he been moved from? Why?
- You've written the number 27 on your board. Why do you think one less than 28 is 27? How might you use the number track to explain to someone who wasn't sure?
- If one more than 68 is 69, what number do you think is one more than 78?

Commentary

This lesson aims to encourage children not only to understand the concept of 'one more than' and 'one less than' but to use this language themselves. As Gifford (2005) points out, some children can tell you one more than/one less than a number but do not necessarily use the language of more than/less than themselves. Children are sometimes expected to understand and use language that they themselves rarely utter, unless it is made part of the activity and, as in the case of this lesson, unless someone else is listening.

The main part of the lesson uses a number track as a representation of the number sequence and offers this as a visual image to support their mathematics. The plenary uses no such image (although there is a suggestion for some children who might need support in 'recording' their answer) and it is hoped that children will be able to identify 'one more than' or 'one less than' a seen number - so there is some level of support, but not as much as in the main part of the lesson. It will be interesting to see whether/which children struggle without the sequence of numbers in sight.

Potential challenges

Children may have more difficulty with identifying 'one less than' than 'one more than'. The language and understanding of 'more than' are likely to be part of their experiences in and out of school; children often have less experience of the idea of 'less than'.

Some children may only be able to identify 'one more than' by counting on, starting from 1. If this is the case, then maybe these children need more experience of counting on from any given start number. It is likely that these children will struggle to identify 'one less than' and these children will need more experience of counting back in ones starting from different numbers. Number tracks can be used to help them to count forwards and backwards.

Ways the lesson could be adapted

The lesson could start with children being given number cards and getting in order, followed by some questioning about which number is one more than or one less than identified numbers. After they have put themselves in order, children could be asked to stand forward if their number is 'one more than . . .' and so on, and continued in this way with 'one less than' introduced through a similar activity. It is important to ask questions in a way that will encourage children to use the appropriate language.

The main part of the lesson could consist of children being given number tracks with some numbers missing and they have to fill in the missing numbers. However, children can sometimes complete this type of activity without engaging with the idea of 'one more than' or 'one less than'; they can simply count their way up and down the number track.

Different number problems can be used with children to apply the ideas of 'one more than' and 'one less than'. For example:

- There are four people on the bus. One more gets on. How many people are now on the bus? It would be important to 'tell the story' using numbers only. One more than four is five, moving on to establishing the number sentences, as described in the next section.

- There are ten children in the toy shop. One goes out. How many children are there now in the shop?

You could ask children to make up stories using the phrases 'one more than' and 'one less than'. This is often a really good way to assess the depth of children's understanding and also give them some ownership of their learning.

How the learning might be developed in future lessons

The learning could be developed into establishing the addition sentences and subtraction sentences that also 'tell the story'. So, saying that 1 more than 7 is 8 is the same story as $7 + 1 = 8$ and 1 less than 30 is the same story as $30 - 1 = 29$, and so on.

Also, important connections can be made. So, for example, if one more than seven is eight, then one less than eight is seven, and although this may seem unnecessary to explore and consolidate, these connections help children to develop important reasoning and logical thinking skills.

At a later stage, similar ideas as those suggested for the lesson could be used to focus on identifying 'ten more than' and 'ten less than' any given number; these are also crucial skills. The use of 1–100 number grids could be a useful resource (see introduction to this chapter) but it is important that children experience adding on and subtracting ten, rather than simply being told to look for the 'number below' or the 'number above'. This is a conclusion they should be encouraged to reach for themselves, with appropriate questioning. If discussion follows as to why this is the case, the relationships between the numbers can be confirmed and children can move on to finding ten more than or ten less than a wider range of numbers.

Key self-evaluation questions to help reflection on practice

- Am I clear about how various images offer different representations of numbers?

- Do I link activity and language for children and do I provide opportunities for children to talk about all of these?

- Do I emphasise the use of reading out loud numbers as well as writing them?

- Do I regularly model my thinking to the children and make connections?

- Do I plan a range of probing questions I can ask during mathematics lessons to help me to assess the depth of children's understanding?

- Do I develop children's understanding of number by encouraging them to visualise numbers in their heads?

Further reading

Briggs, M. (2013) *Teaching and Learning Early Mathematics*. Norwich: Critical Publishing.

Cotton, T. (2013) *Understanding and Teaching Primary Mathematics*. (Chapter 5 – Knowing and using number facts.) Harlow: Pearson.

References

DfE (2013) *The National Curriculum in England Key Stages 1 and 2 Framework Document*. London: Department for Education.

Gifford, S. (2005) *Teaching Mathematics 3–5*. Maidenhead: Open University Press.

Haylock, D. and Cockburn, A. (2008) *Understanding Mathematics for Young Children*. London: Sage.

Chapter 5

Year 2: Place value

Learning outcomes

This chapter will help you to:

- recognise the importance of the accurate use of language when teaching children about place value;
- consider how to develop understanding through using concrete materials, symbols, language and pictures;
- appreciate the importance of encouraging children to visualise numbers in their heads.

Reference to the Teachers' Standards

Working through this chapter will help you meet the following standards:

3. Demonstrate good subject and curriculum knowledge.
4. Plan and teach well-structured lessons.
5. Adapt teaching to respond to the strengths and needs of all pupils.
6. Make accurate and productive use of assessment.

Links to the National Curriculum (DfE, 2013)

Year 2 programme of study (statutory requirements)

Pupils should be taught to:

- recognise the place value of each digit in a two-digit number (tens, ones);
- use place value and number facts to solve problems.

Introduction

Place value and the use of the digits 0–9 to represent all numbers underpins the Hindu–Arabic numeral system that we use today. As adults our number system can appear obvious and straightforward, but this is not always the case for children. You only need to look back in history to some of the advanced civilisations such as the Romans and the Ancient Egyptians to realise that place value was not a concept they had even contemplated when developing their number systems.

In order to understand our number system children need to understand place value. It enables children to read, write and order any number and develop a sense of the size of numbers. It is also crucial when helping children to understand and develop efficient mental and written calculations. Developing children's early understanding of place value is therefore a vital part of the Key Stage 1 curriculum and an insecure understanding is one of the factors that can inhibit their progress into Key Stage 2 and beyond.

To understand our place value system you need to appreciate that:

- there are only ten digits (0–9) and any number can be recorded using these digits;

- the value of each digit in a number is determined by its position in the number;

- zero is used as a place holder, e.g. in 207 the zero shows there are no tens.

To help children appreciate the value of digits, accurate and precise use of language is crucial. When reading a number such as 32 it should always be read out in full ('thirty-two') and not as a list of digits ('three two'). Similarly, a number such as 437 should be read out in full as 'four hundred and thirty-seven'. When talking about a particular digit within a number there are two different ways you can refer to the value of that digit. To use the language of quantity value you would refer to the 3 in 32 as 30 and the 2 as 2. It is also possible to use the language of column value and to do this you would refer to the 3 as 3 tens and the 2 as 2 ones (or units). Typically, quantity value is used within mental calculations strategies and column value within compact vertical-written methods. Thompson (2003) makes the argument that it is not until children are taught compact vertical-written methods that both quantity and column value and the relationship between them need to be understood. For Key Stage 1 and the lesson plan in this chapter the focus is therefore on developing understanding and using the language of quantity value.

Lesson plan

Year 2: Place value	
Focused learning objectives	**Success criteria**
Starter: compare and order numbers from 0 up to 100 **Main:** Recognise the place value (quantity value) of each digit in a two-digit number (tens, ones)	Read two-digit numbers Know that the numbers are in order on a number line or in a hundred grid and use these to help order numbers Know which digit is the tens and which digit is the ones in a given two-digit number Use practical resources and/or images to represent the number of tens and ones in a given two-digit number

Vocabulary

tens, ones, digit, two-digit number, in order, between

Resources

Starter

- Number card for every child (a selection of numbers between 0 and 100 appropriate for the class)
- Set of pre-prepared 'selection' cards and one blank card in a bag, e.g.

More than 40

Between 10 and 20

Less than 50

Main

- Individual whiteboards and pens
- Bags of balloons with ten in each bag (or the lesson context could be changed to another resource that is packaged in tens)
- A set of numbers for each pair of children to use during the main activity (these can be differentiated)

Timing	Starter
10/15 minutes	Take the children out on to the playground. Altogether, rehearse counting in tens and counting in ones from a multiple of ten, e.g. • Count in tens from 0 to 100 • Count in tens from 30 to 80 • Count in ones from 30 to 42

Now give each child a number card so each child has a different number. Explain that you are going to ask some children to get in order. Ask the children to talk to the person next to them to agree what 'in order' means and take feedback. Now choose five children and ask them to see if they can get in order. Ask all the children to watch carefully to see whether they agree. When everyone agrees that the five numbers are correctly placed, choose another five children and ask them to position themselves amongst the numbers already there so that all the numbers are in the right order. Continue to add five children to the line until all numbers have been placed.

Now, using the bag of cards, ask a child to take out one of the cards and read out what is written. The children holding numbers that fit the selection take one step forward. Continue to take out cards from the bag for a few minutes, asking (some) children to justify their step forward. Has everyone taken at least one step forward? If not, ask children to think of what could be written on a card to allow them to move forward. Write this on a card and read it out.

Support

Number lines from 0 to 100 or hundred squares could be available for children to use and check against.

Challenge

What could you write on a selection card that would mean:

• no one steps forward?

• everyone steps forward?

Timing	Main
30 minutes	Introduce the context for the main part of the lesson. Mr Bumble owns a balloon shop. He sells balloons individually and in packs of ten. Explain that we are going to help him with his customers today. The first customer wants 32 balloons. Ask the children in pairs to discuss how many bags and how many individual balloons Mr Bumble needs to give the customer.

Draw three bags and write '10' on each bag and then draw two small balloons and write '1' on each balloon. Count in tens and write '30' underneath the packets and count in ones and write '2' underneath the individual balloons. Now record 30 + 2 = 32:

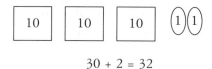

30 + 2 = 32

Now draw two bags and five individual balloons. Ask the children how many balloons this customer has ordered. On whiteboards see if the children can write this calculation (20 + 5 = 25). Repeat the above as necessary and include a 'teens' number. Finally ask the children to close their eyes and try to visualise the number of packets of balloons and individual balloons Mr Bumble will give to the next customer, who wants 43 balloons. Ask the children to draw on their whiteboards what they were seeing in their heads. If there are variations in what the children have drawn, encourage these children to come to the front so you can discuss and show the rest of the class what they have drawn.

Explain that they are now going to work in pairs to help Mr Bumble in his shop. They will take it in turns to be Mr Bumble and the customer. Give each pair a set of numbers you would like them to select from during this activity. The customer will pick one of these numbers and ask for that number of balloons. Mr Bumble will then draw and record the number of balloons the customer will receive (using images and the calculation as above). The customer will try to visualise the number of packets of balloons and individual balloons. The customer must always check that Mr Bumble hasn't made a mistake!

Simplify

Ask the children to count the balloons practically into packets of ten for Mr Bumble. Focus on the teens numbers, e.g. for 13 encourage the children to put ten balloons into a packet and then put three single balloons with it. Encourage the children to describe what they have done to make the required number of balloons.

Extend

Ask the children to work in pairs. Provide them with a sequence of numbers (of balloons) which can be made by adding/removing either tens or ones, e.g. 23 balloons, 27 balloons, 47 balloons, 17 balloons, 12 balloons, 52 balloons, etc.

Explain that there is a difficult customer who keeps changing his mind about how many balloons he wants. Ask them to pick the first number (e.g. 23) and each draw the correct number of packets of balloons and individual balloons. After they have checked each other's drawings they look at the next one on the list (e.g. 27). The customer has changed his mind and now wants a different number of balloons. How can they change their drawing to represent 27? The children must explain to each other what they have done and why, e.g 'I already had 20 balloons and three balloons, which is 23, so I needed to add another four balloons to give me 27'.

	This activity could be recorded in their books or on an activity sheet, with the different numbers shown. This means that changes made are recorded. Try to encourage the children to decide how they might record the changes so that anyone reading their work would be able to follow what they had done.
Timing 10 minutes	**Plenary/conclusion** Write the numbers 23 and 32 on the board. Ask what is the same and what is different about these two numbers? Ask the children to share their ideas with a partner before sharing ideas as a whole class. Ask further questions to probe their understanding, e.g. • How many packets of balloons would I need for 23 balloons? For 32 balloons? • Would you rather be given 23 sweets or 32 sweets? Why? • Would you rather have 23 days or 32 days left until your birthday? Why? • What else can you tell me about number 23?

Assessment opportunities

Whilst they are working, ask children questions such as these. You might want to focus on those children whose level of understanding you are unsure about. These might be children you think are unclear or children whose thinking you can extend.

• Can you explain to my why the picture you've drawn shows 43 balloons?

• This picture shows three bags and four balloons. Would this be right for a customer who asked for 43 balloons? Why?

• This picture shows 43 balloons. If a customer wanted 63 balloons, how many more do you need to give the customer?

• What if a customer wanted 48 balloons but Mr Bumble only has two packets left but lots of single balloons? Can he give the customer what he has asked for? How could he do this? Could we write a numbers sentence to show what this would look like?

Commentary

This lesson aims to make use of a real-life resource to help bridge the gap between the real world and the classroom and to help children see contexts in which is it helpful to recognise tens and ones. Look out for, and encourage the children to find, everyday items that are packaged in tens. You could create an interactive display that encourages children to create a visual representation of numbers using a range of materials either grouped in tens or as individual items; for example you might have interlocking cubes in towers of ten and some everyday objects in groups of ten. To help children gain a broad understanding of place value, you can also integrate many of these contexts into your lessons.

Other particular features of this lesson include:

- using the outside environment;
- developing understanding through concrete materials, symbols, language and pictures;
- visualisation;
- asking related probing questions during the plenary to assess the depth of their understanding.

Mathematics does not have to take place sitting down within the classroom. Working outside and utilising the space that this environment offers can provide more opportunity for children to be active and physically engaged in their learning. In this lesson the outside space gives all of the children room to order themselves. In other lessons you might also look out for mathematics that can be found in the natural and built environment to show children that mathematics is part of the real world. The Council for Learning Outside the Classroom believes that all children should be given the opportunity to experience lessons beyond the classroom walls and actively champion learning outside the classroom to enable children to learn through the real world and hands-on experience (www.lotc.org.uk/about).

The lesson also makes use of concrete materials, symbols, language and pictures. These are the four key components of mathematical experience that Haylock and Cockburn (2008) suggest we can use to help children develop their understanding of number. Within this particular lesson packets of balloons provide the real and concrete materials, the language of quantity value is reinforced throughout, children are encouraged to draw images of the mathematics (by sketching images of the balloons) and they are also encouraged to represent the balloons using mathematical symbols.

Practical and concrete resources are important to mathematics learning as without them the subject can become very abstract. Helping children to internalise images of practical and concrete materials can help them to manipulate them in their minds so that they can still see the mathematics when the resources aren't available. In this lesson children are encouraged to close their eyes, visualise some mathematics and then record what they are seeing. This is also a helpful technique to help you to know what images of mathematics they are beginning to develop.

Questioning is a vital element of mathematics lessons and a few good questions within a lesson plan can help to assess the depth of children's understanding and uncover any misconceptions that may be developing. Within this lesson a key question used in the plenary is, 'What is the same and what is different about these two numbers?' This open question will allow children to make a range of different contributions and provides an opportunity to assess their understanding. It is also a very adaptable question that can be used in lessons that cover other areas of mathematics (e.g. What is the same and what is different about these two shapes?).

Potential challenges

There are some common errors and misconceptions to be aware of when teaching place value.

The 'teens' numbers can be particularly problematic for children. One potential issue is that some of the teens numbers can sound very similar to the tens numbers and so, for example, children may struggle to distinguish between numbers such as forty and fourteen. It is therefore important that both you and the children are very clear and precise when pronouncing numbers.

Recording numbers can also lead to misconceptions and again it is the 'teens' numbers that can cause difficulty. For most two-digit numbers we refer to the tens digit first when saying and recording the number; however, when we say a 'teens' number we refer to the ones digit first. It is therefore not uncommon for children to record numbers such as 'fourteen' as 41. Children also need to appreciate the compact way in which we write all numbers. To some children it is completely logical to write twenty-five as 205 as this matches the way we say the number.

Make sure that you never read a number by just sayings its digits. For example, the number 25 should always be read as 'twenty-five' and not 'two five'.

Ways the lesson could be adapted

- The school hall could be used for the starter instead of the playground (if another class is using it for PE you might be able to have the first few minutes while they get changed).

- Other equipment and contexts could be used instead of the balloons. You could use:

  o 10p and 1p coins to make given amounts;

  o art straws tied together in bundles of ten;

  o everyday items that come in packs of ten;

  o structured place value equipment such as place value (arrow) cards and tens and ones materials.

How the learning might be developed in future lessons

To help children develop a broad and deep understanding of place value, aim to use a wide range of resources, models and images, contexts and recording.

Some of the structured resources, models and images you might use and encourage children to use include place value cards (Figure 5.1), beadstrings and number lines (Figure 5.2), place value charts (Figure 5.3), tens and ones materials (Figure 5.4) and 10p and 1p coins (Figure 5.5).

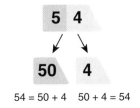

Figure 5.1   Place value cards

Figure 5.2   Beadstrings

100	200	300	400	500	600	700	800	900
10	20	30	40	(50)	60	70	80	90
1	2	3	(4)	5	6	7	8	9

Figure 5.3   Place value charts

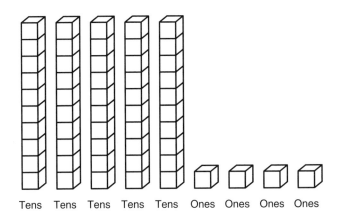

Tens   Tens   Tens   Tens   Tens   Ones   Ones   Ones   Ones

Figure 5.4   Tens and ones materials

Figure 5.5   10p and 1p coins

As children develop their understanding of place value, help them to use it to develop their sense of number by focusing on the relative size of numbers, numbers they fall between, where a number would be positioned on a number line and numbers that come before and after it.

Key self-evaluation questions to help reflection on practice

- Am I clear about the difference between quantity value and column value and do I know when I would use them?

- Am I accurate in my use of language when teaching place value?

- Do I regularly model to the children how the mathematics can be recorded?

- Do I plan a range of probing questions I can ask during mathematics lessons to help me to assess the depth of children's understanding?

- Do I develop children's understanding of number by encouraging them to visualise numbers in their heads?

Further reading

Council for Learning Outside the Classroom (**www.lotc.org.uk/about**)

Haylock, D. and Cockburn, A. (2008) *Understanding Mathematics for Young Children*. London: Sage.

Thompson, I. (2003) Place value: the English disease? Chapter 15 in Thompson I. (ed.) *Enhancing Primary Mathematics Teaching*. Maidenhead: Open University Publications.

References

Council for Learning Outside the Classroom (**www.lotc.org.uk/about**)

DfE (2013) *The National Curriculum in England Key Stages 1 and 2 Framework Document*. London: Department for Education.

Haylock, D. and Cockburn, A. (2008) *Understanding Mathematics for Young Children*. London: Sage.

Thompson, I. (2003) Place value: the English disease? Chapter 15 in Thompson I. (ed.) *Enhancing Primary Mathematics Teaching*. Maidenhead: Open University Publications.

Chapter 6

Year 2: Using ‹ › and = signs

Learning outcomes

This chapter will help you to:

- understand the significance of children creating their own number sentences and identify ways of encouraging children to do this;
- appreciate the importance of children experiencing and talking about ideas before being introduced to new mathematical symbols;
- be aware of some of the difficulties children might experience understanding and using the ‹ and › symbols.

Reference to the Teachers' Standards

Working through this chapter will help you meet the following standards:

2. Promote good progress and outcomes by pupils.
3. Demonstrate good subject and curriculum knowledge.
4. Plan and teach well-structured lessons.
5. Adapt teaching to respond to the strengths and needs of all pupils.
6. Make accurate and productive use of assessment.

Links to the National Curriculum (DfE, 2013)

Year 2 programme of study (statutory requirement)

Pupils should be taught to:

- compare and order numbers from 0 up to 100; use ‹, › and = signs.

Notes and guidance (non-statutory)

Using materials and a range of representations, pupils practise counting, reading, writing and comparing numbers to at least 100 and solving a variety of related problems to develop fluency.

Introduction

This chapter (the lesson plan, together with ideas for how the learning might be extended) aims to use the ideas of less than, equal to and more than, within the notion of comparison and in the context of number. It promotes the aim of using these ideas within 'number sentences', rather than as isolated phrases. The phrases 'less than' and 'more than' are sometimes only used by children in short responses to questions such as, 'Is thirty less than or more than twenty-five?' If we are not careful, we as teachers are the only people in the classroom to utter the complete sentence!

Although the introduction to vocabulary and notation associated with comparison may seem a lengthy process in the lesson described here, it is important that children make sense of these through actively creating, reading and recording their own number sentences. There are many ways of recording comparison and some suggestions are given in the lesson plan. Following the model of learning promoted by Liebeck (1990), where she suggests an experiential → linguistic → pictorial → symbolic progression, children are encouraged to make sense of the idea using words, before they are introduced to the symbols < and > for less than and more than.

Although the phrase 'more than' causes few problems, the phrase 'less than' is not commonly used by children in their everyday conversations. It is therefore important to use situations which 'strongly encourage' the use of this phrase and you will see that this is emphasised throughout the lesson.

Sometimes, children struggle to understand and use the '=' sign as anything other than 'makes', or see it as an instruction to add, subtract, multiply or divide. We want children to understand that it means 'is the same as' and that whatever is either side of the '=' sign must have the same value, even though it may look different. This difficulty may be due to children having limited prior experience and the section on 'How the learning might be developed in future lessons' towards the end of the chapter offers some ideas to broaden their experiences further.

Lesson plan

Year 2: Less than, more than	
Focused learning objectives	**Success criteria**
Starter: Compare two numbers up to 100 **Main:** Use < and > symbols when comparing numbers up to 100	Correctly use the phrases 'is more than' and 'is less than' when comparing two numbers Read, understand and use < and > symbols

Vocabulary
is less than, is smaller than, is more than, is bigger than, between, number sentence

Resources

Starter

- Large number cards (enough for one for each child and one for your use) using a range of numbers from 0 to 100

Main

- Cards with the following phrases (enough for one between two children) and large versions or electronic versions for display

> is less than

> is more than

> is less than
>
> <

> is more than
>
> >

- Set of number cards for you to use, sets of number cards for children to use (any numbers up to 100, choosing appropriate sets for different pairs of children)
- Individual whiteboards and pens

Plenary

- Individual whiteboards and pens
- Strips of coloured paper

Timing	Starter
10/15 minutes	Make sure the children are in a large enough space for them to stand in line and see each other's numbers. Give out large number cards, one per child, and then ask the children to see if they can stand in order, from

smallest to largest. Ask each child to read out their number, asking other children to help out if they struggle. Now take a new card and model positioning yourself in the line.

For example, you might say:

'My number is . . . 47'. Look along the line and find numbers either side of yours. 'My number is more than . . . 38 . . . and it is less than . . . 49 . . . so my number goes here'.

Now ask one child to tell the rest of the class how they know their number is in the right place. They might say, 'My number is 20. 20 is between 16 and 28', or, '20 is bigger than 16 and smaller than 28'. Reinforce the phrase 'more than' and then ask if everyone can think of a sentence for their number using the words 'more than', e.g. 'My number is 20, it is more than 16'. Select some children to take it in turn to say their sentence. For example, 'My number is 56, it is more than 47', or 'My number is 59, it is more than 56', and so on, using the number next to them to compare. Now ask, 'Can we think of a sentence but this time using the words . . . less than'? Model this and give children time to think of a sentence and go along the line of children so that everyone gets a chance to say their number sentence.

Now ask, 'Do we need to use the number next to us?' Model some examples, e.g. if I was 16, I could say, 'My number is 16, it is less than 59'. Ask for some number sentences. It is important that children say these sentences; ask them to say their number sentence to another child and then ask a few to share theirs with the whole class.

Support

Prompt with questions such as:

- What number do you have?
- What number is this number (pointing to a bigger number)? Is your number more than or less than this one? So, 18 is less than 20.

You may need to use 'smaller than/bigger than' alongside 'less than/more than' to help children understand the meaning and the use of 'less than/more than'.

Challenge

Can some children provide number sentences using numbers that are not in the line?

Timing	**Main**
30 minutes	Make sure number cards and 'is less than' cards are on the children's tables, ready for use.

Stage 1

Display the following cards:

6		is less than

and ask someone to read what they can see. 'Six is less than'.

Ask children to select and hold up a number card from their table that would finish the sentence. Choose some of the numbers, one at a time and ask children to read out the full sentence. For example, 'six is less than twelve'. Record some of their suggestions as they are given, to complete the number sentence above. Each time clear and then repeat with the next suggestion.

Now demonstrate how the number cards and the 'is less than' card can be used to make number sentences, starting with different numbers, reading out each time.

Ask children to work in pairs to make number sentences like the ones you have demonstrated. They can take turns to use two number cards and use the 'is less than' card to make number sentences. Explain that they have to read out their number sentence and their partner has to agree it is true before they have their turn to make a new sentence. They can reuse cards.

After 5/10 minutes stop and recap, asking some children to read out a sentence whilst you record for everyone to see.

Now explain that we have a special mathematical symbol for 'is less than'.

is less than
<

Show children the card and draw it so that they can see how you do it. Ask them to copy it in the air. Distribute the cards on to tables so that children can look closely. Now ask them to draw it on their whiteboards and say it as they draw – 'is less than'.

Model how this symbol might be used; for example, you might use some of the sentences children produced earlier. Show some number sentences and ask the children to read them to their partner, e.g.

$3 < 7$ $8 < 20$ $5 < 10$ $23 < 30$

Ask children to create number sentences with their number cards and their symbol cards.

is less than
<

Again, ask them to take turns to use the cards, reading out their sentences and making sure both agree before their partner has a turn.

After 5/10 minutes stop the children and explain that now you are going to ask them to write some number sentences on their whiteboards. Remind them of the ones you showed them earlier (see above). After a few minutes, invite some children to come and share their number sentences with the whole class by writing them on the board, reading them as they do so.

Support

Some children may need to be given smaller numbers and use a number line to decide the order of numbers.

Challenge

Children could be asked to record the number sentences they create. They could then be given perhaps four number cards and a 'is less than' card and asked if they could find all the number sentences possible.

Stage 2

Repeat as above but for 'more than'.

Note: You may decide to leave this stage to another lesson.

Ask children to use their number cards and the 'is more than' card to work in pairs to make number sentences like the ones you have demonstrated. They can take turns to use two number cards and use the 'is more than' card to make number sentences. They have to read out their number sentence and their partner has to agree it is true before they have their turn to make a new sentence.

Now explain that we have a special mathematical symbol for 'is more than' and draw it so they can see how you do it. Ask if they can copy it in the air. Ask if they can draw it on their whiteboards and say it as they draw. Show them a large card (or electronic image) similar to the one below and place it somewhere all children can see it.

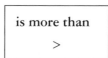

Now show some numbers sentences and ask them to read them to their partner, e.g.

7 > 3   20 > 8   10 > 5   30 > 23

Ask if they can make some number sentences on their whiteboards and then choose some to be read out. Whilst they read out their sentences, record them on the board for all to see.

Timing	Plenary/conclusion
10 minutes	• Explain that you are going to write some number sentences, some of which are true and some of which are not true. Write three or four (e.g. $8 > 3$, $2 < 1$, $4 < 9$). Ask children to talk with their partner and decide which are true and which are false and why. Choose a few children to share their decision with the class and explain why. Try to encourage them to reason, e.g. they may model some counting; they may wish to use a number line to show where the numbers are; they may use a number grid. (Note: If you have only done the first stage of the lesson, just use '<' sentences, making sure some are true and others are false.)
	• Now give children two strips of coloured paper and ask them, in pairs, to write two number sentences, using the < symbol (one on each strip of paper). They should write one number sentence that is true and one that isn't true. Encourage them to put their names on the back and 'True' or 'False'. These can then be collected up and put up on display, with a question, 'True or False?' or they can be used as a starter for another lesson.

Assessment opportunities

Whilst they are working ask children questions such as these. You might want to focus on those children whose level of understanding you are unsure about. These might be children you think are unclear or children whose thinking you can extend.

• Can you read me the sentence you've just made? What other number cards could you put in this place here?

• What if you could use a number that isn't on one of your cards – what could you choose?

• Can you show me where both those numbers are on the number line?

• Suppose someone said, 'thirty-seven is less than thirty' – would they be right? How do you know?

Commentary

The lesson as described here introduces < and > symbols to use when recording the comparison of two numbers. It promotes a gradual introduction and does not expect children to begin to read and use the symbols before exploring and talking about the ideas associated with them. The lesson suggests children work in pairs so that they can read out loud the number sentences they create, first of all using 'long hand', i.e. the actual words, before introducing them to what we might refer to as 'short hand', i.e the symbolic forms.

Potential challenges

Some children may be able to tell you which is the smaller of the two numbers but have difficulty using the correct notation. It is important that in lessons both the children and the teacher continue to use the language alongside the numerals and the notation so that we say the sentence, rather than reduce the mathematics to symbols that are not spoken. As suggested, we may initially need to use the phrases 'less than' and 'more than' alongside language such as 'smaller than' and 'bigger than', but we do want children to progress to understand and use the language of 'less than' and 'more than' so it is important these words are used and children become familiar with them. You may want to use a display to capture the important words, phrases and symbols associated with the ideas in this chapter, maybe with some examples and some questions for children to think about. For example, you may want to include a display of some statements and pose the question – which of these are true?

Sometimes, children mix up the two notations. You may decide to focus on introducing the < symbol in a different lesson from the one where you are introducing the > symbol. Some teachers have ways of helping children to distinguish between them both, often referring to an 'open mouth' as the 'bigger end' of the symbol, so that's where the larger number will be. If children are introduced to such tips, then make sure they have a chance to talk about them, maybe using role play with puppets, for example, to help children make sense and remember them.

Ways the lesson could be adapted

The lesson could be started in an alternative way. You may want to start off the lesson with something such as writing 7 = 9 on the board and ask children what they think. Ask if this is true or not. Ask them to talk to the person next to them and explain why they think it is or isn't true. Take a few responses, asking for a reason each time. Establish from their responses that 7 is less than 9. Remove the '=' sign and ask what we could write here instead. Children may suggest 'smaller than', 'less than', 'is not as big as', 'comes before', and so on. Select 'is less than' and write this between the two numbers. Explain that this sentence is now true.

Ask all children to read the number sentence 'seven is less than nine'. Now remove the numbers 7 and 9 but leave the phrase 'is less than'. Ask them in pairs to suggest some numbers they could use where the sentence is still true, encouraging them to use the language 'is less than'. Ask for some suggestions, insisting that they give the number sentence, not just two numbers. For example, 'eight is less than eleven'.

Now demonstrate how the number cards and 'is less than' card can be used to make number sentences, starting with different numbers, reading out each time. For example, ask two children to pick a number card at random. Ask for their numbers and then ask the class how they think these can be used to make a number sentence using the words 'is less than'. Demonstrate how the cards can be set out. You could proceed to introduce the < symbol and continue to develop the ideas as described in the lesson plan. You may move on to the idea 'more than' and > symbol using the same approach.

The lesson given suggests beginning with developing the idea and notation associated with 'less than'. You may want to develop 'more than' first and then move on to 'less than' and integrate both. There are sound reasons for either route. Children are more familiar with the idea of 'more than' so that may seem a better route to follow, building on language they are already familiar with and use. However, they frequently see numbers in order of increasing magnitude and would readily position numbers so that a smaller one would be positioned to the left of a larger one, if asked to put them in order. So, whatever we choose, they have experiences on which we can build.

You could use money or measurement for the context of this lesson. For example, without seeing the coins, two children collect money from a bag of 10p and 1p coins. They then look at their coins and work out who has less. Children can record using cards and money, then maybe record as 13p < 22p, following the example shown in Figure 6.1.

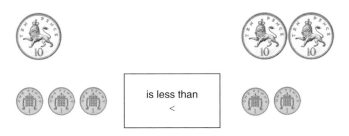

Figure 6.1   Coin comparison

How the learning might be developed in future lessons

You can provide opportunities for children to extend the idea of comparison of numbers by incorporating addition and/or subtraction sentences into their learning and making more use of the '=' sign as meaning 'is the same as', as mentioned in the introduction to this chapter.

You could begin by asking children to write '5 = 5' on their individual whiteboards (one between two children). Now, taking it in turns, they rub out one side of the equation and replace it with something of the same value. For example, rub out 5 on the left side and replace with '2 + 3', so the board now looks like '2 + 3 = 5'. The next person rubs out the right-hand side and replaces it with something different to what is already written. For example, rub out 5 and replace with 1 + 1 + 3, so now the board looks like '2 + 3 = 1 + 1 + 3', and so on. This needs careful modelling before children work in pairs but the idea is something that can be extended for different operations and for a wide variety of numbers. Also, you might want to model it for 5 = 5 and then ask children to apply it to 6 = 6, for example. You can set a challenge to suit the needs of your groups/pairs. This type of activity can be used right up to Year 6 (and beyond)!

It is important to ask the children to read out their 'sentences' following each turn.

These sorts of activities reinforce the meaning of the '=' sign and provide a good foundation from which children can build their understanding of equations.

You may want to replace the '=' sign with < or > symbol and proceed as above. So, the 'board story' may go as follows:

$4 < 5$

$2 + 2 < 5$

$2 + 2 < 3 + 2$

The ones shown above maintain a value of 5 on the right-hand side and a value of 4 on the left-hand side of the inequality.

You could also build on the idea of linking both 'less than' and 'more than'. If we know, for example, that 56 > 23 then we also know that 23 < 56. This is implicit in the mathematics we have explored but children can make the connection and make it explicit with discussion and number sentences they can create.

Key self-evaluation questions to help reflection on practice

- Do I encourage children to create their own number sentences?

- Do I provide the opportunity for children to explore mathematical ideas before introducing them to new mathematical symbols?

- Do I encourage children to read out loud number sentences as well as write them?

- Do I regularly model to the children how the mathematics can be recorded?

- Do I plan a range of probing questions I can ask during mathematics lessons to help me to assess the depth of children's understanding?

- Do I develop children's understanding of number by encouraging them to visualise numbers in their heads?

- Do I sometimes provide them with true and false statements and ask them to decide which are which and to explain how they know?

Further reading

Cockburn, A. and Littler, M. (2008) *Mathematical Misconceptions*. (Chapter 7 – Equality: getting the right balance.) London: Sage.

References

DfE (2013) *The National Curriculum in England Key Stages 1 and 2 Framework Document*. London: Department for Education.

Liebeck, P. (1990) *How Children Learn Mathematics*. London: Penguin.

Chapter 7

Year 3: Patterns when counting in multiples

Learning outcomes

This chapter will help you to:

- consider possible ways to enrich children's experience and understanding of multiples;
- value the importance of regularly reinforcing the mathematical vocabulary you want children to use and remember;
- appreciate how children need time to explore and identify patterns in number.

Reference to the Teachers' Standards

Working through this chapter will help you meet the following standards:

2. Promote good progress and outcomes by pupils.
3. Demonstrate good subject and curriculum knowledge.
4. Plan and teach well-structured lessons.
6. Make accurate and productive use of assessment.

Links to the National Curriculum (DfE, 2013)

Year 3 programme of study (statutory requirements)

Pupils should be taught to:

- count from 0 in multiples of 4, 8, 50 and 100;
- recall and use multiplication and division facts for the 3, 4 and 8 multiplication tables.

Notes and guidance (non-statutory)

Pupils now use multiples of 2, 3, 4, 5, 8, 10, 50 and 100.

Introduction

The National Curriculum (DfE, 2013) states that *By the end of year 4, pupils should have memorised their multiplication tables up to and including the 12 multiplication table and show precision and fluency in their work.* If we rely on learning multiplication tables by memorisation alone then to know up to 12×12 can involve learning 144 isolated facts. Bird (2011) discusses how children who struggle with mathematics often have difficulties in reliably remembering and memorising facts. Therefore to support children we can help them to recognise that facts are not isolated and to see how patterns and connections can be used. Haylock (2010, p25) describes this process as *constructing a network of connections, which helps me to make sense of these numbers, to see patterns and use relationships.* This takes time and therefore opportunities need to be provided to enable children to explore patterns and connections for themselves.

Counting in multiples is included in the National Curriculum programmes of study (DfE, 2013) and can be seen as one way of supporting the understanding and knowledge of multiplication tables. This lesson is designed to help children to explore and identify patterns whilst counting in multiples so that this can enrich their experience and understanding of multiples and ultimately support them as they develop their sense of number.

Lesson plan

Year 3: Patterns when counting in multiples	
Focused learning objectives	**Success criteria**
Starter: Use multiplication facts for the 2, 3, 5 and 10 multiplication tables	Describe a pattern made by multiples of 4
Main: Explore patterns in multiples of 4 and 8	Describe a pattern made by multiples of 8

Vocabulary
number sentence, multiple, digit, units digit, times, groups of, lots of, commutative

Resources
Starter
• Individual whiteboards and pens for the children
Main
• Copies of 'multiples of 4' table and 'multiples of 8' table for children who may have difficulty generating this format independently (see example in the main part of the lesson)
• Copies of digit wheels the children can use for recording
• Multiplication grids (see Models, images and practical resources section at the back of this book) to support children who are struggling to recall multiples of 4 or 8

Timing	Starter/introduction
10/15 minutes	Write the following numbers randomly on the board:
	2 3 5 10 15 20
	Ask the children to choose three of the numbers to make a multiplication number sentence.
	How many different number sentences can they record on their whiteboards?
	Invite contributions from the children and write their responses systematically on the board, e.g.
	$2 \times 5 = 10$ $2 \times 10 = 20$ $3 \times 5 = 15$
	$5 \times 2 = 10$ $10 \times 2 = 20$ $5 \times 3 = 15$
	Ask children why they think you have recorded them in pairs. Take feedback.
	Explain that when you multiply two numbers together it does not matter which number comes first (you may want to let the class know that because of this, mathematicians say that multiplication is commutative). Draw an array/grid on the board to reinforce this.

For example, Figure 7.1 shows not only 2 rows of 5 but also 5 columns of 2.

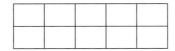

Figure 7.1 An array

You may also want to show them a pegboard arrangement and demonstrate rotating the board through 90 degrees.

Now ask the children if they can think of and record other pairs of multiplication number sentences that have an answer of 20. This time record these randomly on the board and then ask children to identify pairs of calculations to show that multiplication is commutative.

Finally pick one of the number sentences, e.g. 4 × 5 = 20, and ask the children to think about and discuss with their partner different ways of reading the number sentence, e.g.

- 4 multiplied by 5 equals 20
- 4 five times equals 20
- 4 lots of 5 equals 20
- 4 times 5 equals 20
- 20 equals four times five

Take feedback.

Timing	Main
30 minutes	Explain that in the lesson they are going to explore multiples and their patterns.
	Ask the children in pairs to remind each other what a multiple is and to be ready to say to the whole class a sentence using the word 'multiple'. Take feedback from different pairs of children and then agree on a class definition.
	To check for misconceptions and to assess the depth of their understanding ask questions such as:
	<ul><li>I'm going to start at 1 and count in threes: 1, 4, 7, 10 . . . I'm counting in threes, so am I saying numbers which are multiples of 3? Why/Why not?</li><li>What numbers is 10 a multiple of (1, 2, 5, 10)? Why?</li><li>Ask children, in pairs, to pick another number and write all of the numbers it is a multiple of. Take feedback, asking children to speak in sentences using the word multiple, e.g. 8 is a multiple of 1, 2, 4 and 8.</li></ul>

Explain that in this lesson they are going to explore patterns in multiples to see how that might help them to recognise multiples of different numbers. Model, using multiples of 2, the activity you would like them to explore. Quickly complete the grid in Figure 7.2 with the support of the children (you could count together as a class or you could target individuals to fill in some of the gaps). Complete the 'multiples of 2' row first and then identify the 'units digit' in each number and record it in the bottom row.

	1	2	3	4	5	6	7	8	9	10	11	12
Multiples of 2	2	4	6	8	10	12	14	16	18	20	22	24
The units digits	2	4	6	8	0	2	4	6	8	0	2	4

Figure 7.2 Completing the grid

Once the 'units digits' have been recorded ask what the children notice. Do they see a pattern? Show how you can make a diagram of this pattern by recording this visually using the digit wheel (Figure 7.3: e.g. draw a line to join the numbers in order from the row of 'units digits' in Figure 7.2, from 2 to 4, then from 4 to 6, then from 6 to 8, etc.).

What shape do they see? Establish that this pattern creates a pentagon.

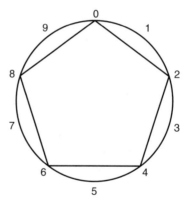

Figure 7.3 Digit wheel

Explain that you would like them to explore the digits that multiples of 4 end in and multiples of 8 end in. Quickly as a class count in 4s and then 8s and then explain that you would like them to complete a table before recording the outcome on a digit wheel. Do they think they will also make pentagons or will the unit numbers join together to make a different shape?

Reinforce that the lesson is all about multiples so this is a key word you expect them to be using throughout the rest of the lesson.

	Simplify
	Provide the children with a resource to help them to complete the multiples of 4 and multiples of 8 tables if appropriate (e.g. a multiplication square).
	Extend
	The enquiry could be extended by considering the patterns in the units digit and the shapes made on the digit wheel when exploring other multiples, e.g. multiples of 3, 6 and 9.
	Alternatively, the children could be challenged to explore multiples of 4 with larger numbers, e.g. give them the following statement: 'If the last two digits in a number are multiples of 4 then the number is a multiple of 4. Is this statement sometimes, always or never true?'
Timing 10 minutes	**Plenary/conclusion** Start the plenary by asking the children to get into pairs and to tell each other what patterns they noticed whilst exploring multiples of 4 and multiples of 8. Share all of the patterns the children noticed. Now ask them to use this information to answer questions such as: • Can a multiple of 4 ever end in a 7? How do you know? • Can 187 be a multiple of 8? How do you know? • If I know that the 13th multiple of 4 ends in a 2, what must the 14th multiple of 4 end in? Why? • 100 is a multiple of 4. Can you tell me some multiples of 4 bigger than 100? Finally ask the whole class to count in 2s, 4s and 8s, emphasising the units digit as they do so to reinforce the pattern you would like them to go away and try to remember.

Assessment opportunities

Whilst they are working ask children questions such as these:

• How can you describe the patterns you have found?

• How does this help you to predict what the next number would be?

• Can you now tell me a number that can't be a multiple of 4? How do you know?

Commentary

Two particular features of this lesson include:

• developing children's understanding and accurate use of mathematical vocabulary;

• exploring patterns in number.

(Continued)

(Continued)

If we want children to talk about mathematics then we need to give them the vocabulary to do so; for example, it is much harder to describe two perpendicular lines if you don't know the word 'perpendicular'. Technical mathematical language can be used infrequently and as a result can become difficult to remember. We therefore need to provide regular and planned opportunities to engage children in using the language of mathematics within mathematics lessons. While it is important for children to listen to the teacher using appropriate mathematical vocabulary this alone is not enough. To gain confidence children also need to use the words and phrases within the context of the lesson. Within this lesson children have the opportunity to discuss the word 'multiple' with a partner before sharing ways in which it can be used within a sentence. This not only provides a good opportunity to assess their understanding but it also enables the class to hear the word used in a variety of sentences and contexts. It is also an interesting word to focus on as it has an everyday meaning as well as a mathematical meaning. In everyday life it can mean 'several' whilst in mathematics it has a very specific link to multiplication.

As teachers it is important to be aware of words with multiple meanings so that potential difficulties can be anticipated in mathematics. Think about some of the following words that are used in mathematics that children may have also encountered with a different meaning in everyday life: odd, face, difference, table, volume, product and take-away. You may want to consider buying a mathematics dictionary, using an online version or involve the children in adding their own entries into a class dictionary you develop throughout the year.

Buchanan (no date) describes mathematics as the study of pattern. When exploring multiples and multiplication tables there are some obvious and some less obvious patterns that can help to lessen the burden of memorising so many individual facts. Our place value system helps children to realise that multiples of ten only produce numbers that end with zero whilst counting in fives produces a pattern of units digits that alternate between 5 and 0. This lesson helps children to recognise that other patterns also exist when exploring other multiples and these can be represented in different ways. In this example they are represented visually using the idea of a digit wheel.

Potential challenges

For children who are having significant difficulties in remembering sequences of multiples and multiplication facts you can give them access to a multiplication square. However it is important that they understand how the numbers on the grid have been generated in the first place. You could therefore initially give them a blank multiplication grid and support them to generate and record the numbers for themselves. They may not necessarily have to do this for the full grid but by completing some of it they will have more understanding of what the numbers on the grid signify.

Ways the lesson could be adapted

There are many other patterns and connections that could also be explored. For children who are able to double numbers they can explore how doubling multiples of 2 produces multiples of 4 and doubling them again produces multiples of 8. Hundred squares can be a useful resource that can be used to explore horizontal, vertical and diagonal patterns in multiples. For example children could shade the multiples of 4 up to 40 and then use the pattern to predict whether larger numbers on the hundred square are also multiples of 4. Alternatively they could shade two sets of multiples such as multiples of 4 and multiples of 8 and establish which numbers are shaded twice and why. For children who already have a fluent understanding and knowledge of multiples of four they could be asked to extend this knowledge to derive multiples of 40 or even 400.

How the learning might be developed in future lessons

Other patterns, such as those noted above, could be used to reinforce and further develop children's appreciation of patterns in number. To support their learning of multiplication tables further throughout Years 3 and 4, aim to introduce children to a wide variety of strategies they can use. For example you could consider:

- using rhymes or multiplication songs to put them into a memorable context;

- asking the children to make their own flashcards or posters so they have something personal they can refer to regularly;

- playing matching games such as Pelmanism or snap;

- helping children recognise how knowing one multiplication fact can help them to derive others, e.g. how knowing 10×4 can help you work out 9×4.

Key self-evaluation questions to help reflection on practice

- Do I regularly reinforce the vocabulary that I want children to remember and use within mathematics lessons?

- Do I expect children to make use of identified vocabulary during mathematics lessons?

- Do I reinforce mathematical vocabulary by asking children to read number sentences in different ways?

- In some mathematics lessons do I expect children to answer in full sentences or put identified mathematical vocabulary into full sentences?

- Do I give children the opportunity to explore multiples and multiplication facts during the main part of mathematics lessons and not just as starter activities?

- Do I provide children with time to explore and identify patterns in number?

Further reading

DfEE (1999) *Mathematical Vocabulary*. Suffolk: DfEE Publications.

References

Bird, R (2011) *The Dyscalculia Resource Book*. London: Sage.

Buchanan, M (no date) *Pattern Power* (online). Available from **http://nrich.maths.org/2148**

DfE (2013) *The National Curriculum in England Key Stages 1 and 2 Framework Document*. London: Department for Education.

Haylock, D. (2010) *Mathematics Explained for Primary Teachers*. London: Sage.

Chapter 8

Year 4: Negative numbers

Learning outcomes

This chapter will help you to:

- consider ways in which children might be introduced to negative numbers;
- recognise the value of using games as part of children's learning and to be aware of features to be considered;
- understand the importance of using a number line to position numbers and to relate them to others.

Reference to the Teachers' Standards

Working through this chapter will help you meet the following standards:

2. Promote good progress and outcomes by pupils.
3. Demonstrate good subject and curriculum knowledge.
4. Plan and teach well-structured lessons.
5. Adapt teaching to respond to the strengths and needs of all pupils.
6. Make accurate and productive use of assessment.

Links to the National Curriculum (DfE, 2013)

Year 4 programme of study (statutory requirements)

Pupils should be taught to:

- count backwards through zero to include negative numbers;
- solve number and practical problems that involve . . . the above.

Introduction

The idea of using negative numbers might seem obvious and logical to us but this has not always been the case. Many ancient civilisations thought negative answers to calculations were meaningless and it wasn't until the seventeenth century that negative numbers were thought to have their uses. It was a mathematician in the seventeenth century, John Wallis, who was the first person to think of the idea of a number line using negative numbers (Howard, no date).

The ideas in this chapter are based around the order of numbers using a number line. Children should already be familiar with number lines to identify position and relative size of positive numbers so it makes sense to extend the number line beyond zero to incorporate negative numbers. In the main part of the lesson it is important to give children time to look at the number line and talk about it, rehearse the way the numbers are spoken and start to understand why −6 is less than −5, although 6 is more than 5, for example.

We can associate 'below zero' or 'less than zero' with various contexts. You may have done some work in science which has involved measuring temperatures and/or talked about the freezing point of water, so bring this into your introduction as appropriate.

When teaching children about negative numbers it is important to consider the vocabulary used. When reading temperature many people refer to temperatures below zero as 'minus . . .'. When reading negative numbers on a number line, they should however be read as 'negative one, negative two' and so on. It is important that we use the correct terminology and encourage children to do the same. The word 'minus' is linked with the operation of subtraction so it is best avoided when talking about numbers less than zero.

Lesson plan

Year 4: Negative numbers	
Focused learning objectives	**Success criteria**
Starter: Recognise the use of negative numbers **Main:** Order whole numbers, including negative numbers	Recognise when negative numbers might be used Count backwards through zero to include negative numbers Use a number line to identify numbers which are less than or more than given positive or negative numbers Order whole numbers, including negative numbers

Vocabulary

negative numbers, below zero, less than zero, thermometer, temperature, consecutive numbers

Resources

Starter

- Large image(s) of thermometers, showing a temperature range to include negative numbers

Main

- Large horizontal number line showing numbers from −20 to 20
- Table-top number lines showing numbers from −20 to 20
- Instruction cards for Capture Three activity – see Figure 8.1
- Counters
- Individual whiteboards and pens

A number less than −17	A number bigger than 10	A number bigger than −4	A number between 0 and −5	A number between 2 and −2	A number between 1 and −10
A number less than −10	A number more than −3	A number less than 4	A number between −3 and 6	A number more than −19	A number less than −5

Figure 8.1 Cards for Capture Three activity

Plenary

- Set of shuffled number cards from −19 to 10 (if there are 30 children in the class). You may need to adjust the number needed for your class, so that each child can be given a different number card

Timing	Starter/introduction
10/15 minutes	Display an image of a thermometer (ideally an interactive version where the temperature can be changed; if not, one where the temperature can be marked and cleared).
	Ask children to discuss in pairs what they can see, what they think it is and how they think it works.
	Take feedback and establish that it is an image of a thermometer. It is used to measure temperature and the display changes according to the temperature. Set or display a temperature to show the likely temperature inside the classroom. Ask children to read the thermometer.
	Now ask what will happen as the temperature falls and the thermometer is placed outside on a cold winter's night. Indicate the falling temperature until it gets to zero, asking the children to read the numbers as you go. Ask them to discuss in pairs whether the temperature can go below zero. Agree that it can. Zero means that it would be at the point of freezing. Ask children to talk to their partner about what happens below zero. Take feedback and establish that there are numbers below zero. At this stage accept the terminology 'minus one, minus two, . . .' but introduce the terminology 'negative one, negative two . . .' as another way of describing these numbers, and write the word 'negative' for the class to see.
	Support
	Provide images of thermometers for small groups/individuals to use, so that they can make closer inspection.
	Challenge
	Can children write down temperatures that are lower than −10 degrees? When/where might this temperature be experienced?
Timing	Main
30 minutes	Display the −20 to 20 number line. Now ask children to work in pairs and to say three things each that they notice, taking turns to say one thing at a time. Collect in various responses, acknowledging what they say and encouraging children to use the word 'negative' when referring to numbers less than zero. For example, 'Yes, minus five, or negative five, is the same distance from zero as five. Shall we try to use the word negative when we are talking about a number that is less than zero?'
	Some of the responses might include:
	• zero is in the middle
	• it's like the thermometer
	• it doesn't start with zero

- negative five is the same distance from zero as five
- it's like the other number lines we use but has extra numbers on it
- the smallest number is negative 20
- the numbers 'match' on both sides of zero
- −1 and 1 are either side of zero
- the negative numbers look as if they should be getting bigger going further away from zero
- as you go right, numbers get bigger; as you go left, numbers get smaller

although children may come up with a range of other comments, some of which might be less mathematical!

Now explain that you are all going to count backwards along the number line starting from the biggest number and counting down to the smallest. Start at 20 and, pointing to each number in turn, count in ones until you get to −20. Now explain that you are going to start with the smallest number and count up. Start at −20 and count along the number line until you get to 20.

Explain to children that they are going to be 'number finders' and they are going to work in pairs. Ask them to write down their answers on their whiteboards. Ask a variety of questions that encourage them to find numbers on the number line that fit with your challenge. Try to use a variety of language (e.g. bigger than, more than, less than, smaller than).

For example:

- Find me a number that is less than three.
- Find me a number that is more than negative six.
- Find me a number that is smaller than zero.
- Find me a number that is bigger than negative fifteen.
- Find me a number that is between negative seven and zero.

After each question, take some feedback and ask children to justify their answers, maybe coming out to use the number line and explain why the number they have found fits with your challenge.

Other types of questions might be:

- What if someone gave . . . as a number to fit with the challenge? Would they be right? Why/Why not?
- Why are there several numbers that fit the challenge?

Now explain that you would like them to work in pairs with their own number line and play Capture Three.

	Model the activity first with one child and yourself. You need some counters each, a different colour for each player. The instruction cards are shuffled and placed face down. You take it in turns to turn over a card and read the instruction. For example, smaller than −3 (read as smaller than negative three). The person who has turned over that card needs to place one of his/her counters on any number on the number line which fits with the instruction on the card. The activity carries on this way but each person is trying to get three of their counters in a line, on three consecutive numbers. Once a number has been 'captured', it cannot be held by anyone else (i.e. two counters are not allowed on the same number).
	There may be times when a card is turned over and a player cannot place a counter. The player has to miss a turn. If the pile of cards has been used and the game is not over, cards can be shuffled and used again. Sometimes the game might be drawn, if no one can manage to capture three in a row. You can modify the game as appropriate.
	Support
	The instructions on the cards can be simplified, restricted to 'less than' or 'more than' instructions or maybe use a smaller range. For example, use numbers within the range −10 to 10.
	Challenge
	This game can be played at different levels so can be self-differentiated without losing the purpose of becoming familiar with using negative numbers. Some children will play more strategically than others when placing their counters.
	Also, after the game has been played the players can then be asked to make their own set of instruction cards and try them out. Sets of different instruction cards can be swapped amongst pairs of children.
Timing 10 minutes	**Plenary/conclusion** You could do this activity in the classroom if you have space or you could go into the hall or outside if the weather is kind! Plenty of space means that the children can move around easily. Distribute number cards to children and ask them to get themselves in order, starting with the smallest number. Try not to interfere! When they have done this, ask them to check with the number either side and be convinced they are in the correct position. Now ask them to say their numbers in order and ask everyone to listen carefully to see if all the numbers are in the correct position. Now, provide some instructions and ask that anyone who has a number that fits with your instruction steps forward.

Ask as many instructions as you have time for. Instructions might be:

- Step forward if your number is smaller than negative 11.
- Step forward if your number is bigger than 13.
- Step forward if your number is between negative 14 and 6.

Each time, ask others to make sure the correct numbers have stepped forward.

If you have time, you could ask the children to give instructions too.

Ask children if they can think of a question which would mean:

- everyone steps forward?
- no one steps forward?

Assessment opportunities

Whilst they are working ask children questions such as these. You might want to focus on those children whose level of understanding you are unsure about. These might be children you think are unclear or children whose thinking you can extend.

- You've covered up that number with your counter. Without moving your counter, can you tell me what that number is? How did you know?
- Could you read out to me all the numbers on your number line that are less than negative 4?
- Can you tell me another number that is less than negative 4?
- Can you tell me all the numbers on your number line that are between negative 3 and 0?
- What number would you like to cover next? Why?
- If you could write your own card next, what would you write? Why?

Commentary

The lesson makes use of a real-life context to introduce negative numbers and moves to an extension of the number line to help develop children's understanding. It is important that children have time to compare a number line that includes negative numbers to ones they are already familiar with and make some observations before they are asked to use it. This lesson uses a game as an activity to make sense and then consolidate children's learning. Games can be a useful way of engaging children and having purpose. If games are to be as beneficial as they can be, we need to ensure we include certain features. Examples might be:

(Continued)

(Continued)

- Do a whole-class/group demonstration first.
- Ask children, in pairs, to talk over the rules before paired/group play begins and ask someone to say what they are, to the whole class. Address any confusion/ misunderstandings.
- Make one of the rules one that involves children talking to each other about what they are doing/have done (for example, in the game above, children might say, 'the card says number less than negative three . . . I am choosing negative five to put my counter on ').
- The partner has to agree/disagree with the outcome of each stage before play continues, providing a reason for disagreement, if this is the case.
- Ask children to reflect on the game, e.g. Which parts were difficult? What did they think they were learning? How could the game be changed?

You can modify games to suit different needs or aspects of mathematics. The Capture Three game described in the lesson could be adapted in many ways, for different sets of numbers, different sets of instruction cards, and so on.

The game in this lesson involves children reading instructions, using the correct vocabulary and making judgements about which numbers fit with what they've been asked for.

Children are asked to talk and work in pairs at several stages of the lesson and there is very little recording, other than a small amount of use of their whiteboards. At this early stage of working with negative numbers, it is important children read and say the numbers, locate the numbers on the number line and begin to recognise the order and position of negative numbers. Shared activities allow for discussion and any disagreement or lack of clarity can be addressed, although some situations might still need support from others.

Children are asked to make a 'human number line' in the plenary and it is suggested that this be done outdoors. Children have the space to move around and it offers another environment in which mathematics can be carried out.

Potential challenges

Many children seem to take on the idea that numbers extend beyond zero quite happily, and can label points beyond zero. Some children find it difficult to understand that, for example, negative seven is less than negative six, because seven is more than six. It is important to continue to use the number line where these numbers can be seen in relation to each other and in relation to zero.

Some children hesitate when using the language of 'negative' when referring to numbers less than zero. This is understandable; many adults use the word 'minus' but we can help to reinforce this by modelling its use and by having classroom displays using this terminology. The children are required to use this vocabulary themselves during the lesson; we must ensure they do this. We might want children to revisit the vocabulary and associated ideas from time to time; children do forget language if they don't use it often.

Ways the lesson could be adapted

For the introduction, there are various contexts that could be used. For example, you might use the context of a multistory building with levels above and below ground or a swimming pool with steps or a ladder which has rungs above the water and below the water, or a sea context and use the notion of height above or below sea level.

You could use the instructions cards to play bingo. The children choose, say, ten numbers between −20 and 20 and write them down in their own grid. You can then call out instructions (similar to the ones provided for the main part of the lesson) one at a time and they cross off any one number that fits the instruction. The first person to cross them all out is the winner.

A set of cards, numbered from −15 to 5, could be provided for pairs of children and they could be asked to put them in order, starting with the smallest. They then read them out. Next, one child closes their eyes whilst the other turns over one of the cards. The partner then opens their eyes and has to work out what number has been turned over. The children take turns to do this.

Play the game Higher or Lower. For a whole-class game you could provide a set of number cards with a selection of positive and negative numbers on them. Show all the cards to the children and ask them to say the number to the person next to them. This is just to make sure they know all of the numbers being used. The numbers can be placed in an envelope or in a bag. Ask a child to take one out of the bag, show it to the rest of the class and ask what number it is and place it on the board (e.g. −1). Now ask whether they think the next number to be taken out of the bag will be higher or lower than the number on the board. Ask them to write H or L on their whiteboards, depending on their decision, and then hold up their boards. Ask another child to take out a new card from the bag and establish whether it is higher or lower than the number on the board. You may want to refer to the number line to justify the answer, or you may want children to do this. Place the new card either to the left or to the right of the card on the board, depending on whether the number is lower or higher than the card already on the board. Now remove the original card placed on the board. The game continues in this way, each time placing the newly chosen card on the board and removing the previous one. You can introduce a scoring system if you wish, so children might put a tick on their whiteboards each time they guess right, for example.

How the learning might be developed in future lessons

Make use of data from a variety of sources (e.g. newspapers, internet) where temperatures of places around the world can be found. The information might be given as a daily update or found when looking at annual/seasonal temperatures. You can ask questions such as:

- Where was the coldest place on this list? What was the temperature?

- How many places recorded a temperature below zero?

- Which places recorded a temperature between … and … ?

You could position a chart for classroom display and accompany it with some questions for children to think about and maybe write their answers.

Using a number line similar to the one used in the main activity, children could count up or down a specific number of 'steps' from given starting numbers. For example, starting at 4, count back 6, and identify the finish number. This could be developed into a game for two or more, where children place counters on 0, take turns to reveal cards which give them an instruction (e.g. move forwards 3, move backwards 5, move forwards 1, etc.) and move their counter accordingly. The first player to reach a certain point (e.g. either end of the number line, or +15, or −15, or −10, or …) or the person who is furthest away from 0 after ten cards each is the winner. Children can play your version of the game first and then make up their own rules.

Key self-evaluation questions to help reflection on practice

- Do I ask children to read out numbers as well as write them?

- Do I relate numbers to their position on the number line and in relation to other numbers?

- Do I regularly model to the children the language of mathematics?

- Do I plan a range of probing questions I can ask during mathematics lessons to help me to assess the depth of children's understanding?

- Do I ask children to think of their own questions?

- Do I provide opportunity for children to justify their answers?

- Do I develop children's understanding of number by encouraging them to visualise numbers in their heads?

Further reading

Haylock, D. (2010) *Mathematics Explained*. (Chapter 16 – Integers: positive and negative.) London: Sage.

References

DfE (2013) *The National Curriculum in England Key Stages 1 and 2 Framework Document*. London: Department for Education.

Howard, J. (no date) *Negative Numbers* (online). Available from: **http://nrich.maths.org/5747**

Chapter 9

Year 4: Roman numerals

Learning outcomes

This chapter will help you to:

- consider how different number systems operate;
- recognise the importance of place value in the number system we use;
- appreciate how discussion in pairs, small groups and the whole class can provide different forums for children to explain their thinking.

Reference to the Teachers' Standards

Working through this chapter will help you meet the following standards:

3. Demonstrate good subject and curriculum knowledge.
4. Plan and teach well-structured lessons.
5. Adapt teaching to respond to the strengths and needs of all pupils.
6. Make accurate and productive use of assessment.

Links to the National Curriculum (DfE, 2013)

Year 4 programme of study (statutory requirements)

Pupils should be taught to:

- read Roman numerals to 100 (I to C) and know that, over time, the numeral system changed to include the concept of zero and place value.

Year 4 programme of study notes and guidance (non-statutory)

- Roman numerals should be put in their historical context so pupils understand that there have been different ways to write whole numbers and that the important concepts of zero and place value were introduced over a period of time.

Introduction

The Romans used letters of the alphabet in order to record their numerals: I (1), V (5), X (10), L (50), C (100), D (500) and M (1 000). Their system was built around a principle in which numbers were written by adding together the value of the numerals and then recording these in descending order. For example, 16 would be recorded as XVI (10 + 5 + 1) and not as IVX (1 + 5 + 10). To ensure some consistency in how they recorded numbers the Romans also used the following rules:

- Numbers were written using as few numerals as possible.

- The biggest-value numerals possible should be used (so 12 would be recorded as XII and not VVII).

- To try and prevent very long numbers, one smaller numeral could be used to the left of a larger numeral to indicate that this value was subtracted. This enabled a number such as 19 to be recorded as IXX (10 + 10 − 1) rather than XVIIII (10 + 5 + 1 + 1 + 1 + 1).

The Roman numeral system did not include zero. It was the Indian and Arab mathematicians after the end of the Roman Empire who invented our present Hindu–Arabic numeral system, where we use the positional concept of 'place value' and have a symbol representing zero to show an empty place/column. It was much easier to calculate using the Hindu–Arabic system and so this system gradually replaced the use of Roman numerals. However we have never fully stopped using Roman numerals, as even today they are used on clock faces, for page numbers in introductions to books, when naming Popes and monarchs (e.g. Henry VIII), to record the years in which films and television programmes were produced and in sporting events (e.g. the summer 2012 Olympics was officially known as the Games of the XXX Olympiad).

The purpose of the following lesson is to explore with children how a very different number system operates and to use this experience to help children to recognise some of the features of the Hindu–Arabic system we use today. In particular it is hoped that the children will appreciate the importance of zero and its role as a place holder (e.g. in 207 the zero shows there are no 'tens') and that, in our system, the value of each digit in a number is determined by its position within the number.

Lesson plan

Year 4: Roman numerals	
Focused learning objectives	**Success criteria**
Starter: Recognise the place value of each digit in a four-digit number (thousands, hundreds, tens and units/ones) **Main:** Read Roman numerals to 100 (I to C) and know that, over time, the numeral system changed to include the concept of zero and place value	Be familiar with the letters that the Romans used to represent numbers Understand the rules the Romans used to write numbers 1–100 Understand some of the differences between the number system we use today and the system the Romans used

Vocabulary
numeral, number, place value, place holder, digit, one-digit number, two-digit number, three-digit number, four-digit number

Resources
Starter

- Individual whiteboards and pens for the children

Main

- Large sheets of sugar paper split into a ten by two grid as shown in Figure 9.1 (these will combine in the plenary to make one big hundred square containing Roman numerals)

Figure 9.1   Ten by two grid

Plenary

- A large 1–100 square (so children can compare and contrast Roman numerals with our number system)

Timing	Starter/introduction
15 minutes	Write the following three numbers on the board: 4 205 4 025 4 052 Make sure the children can read each number and then ask them to discuss in pairs which number is the odd one out and why. Encourage them to find reasons why each number could be the odd one out and to be ready to justify their reasoning. Take feedback, making sure that comments made about the place value of the digits in the number are discussed. The following questions can help to elicit specific information if it is not part of the initial feedback:

- What does the 4 represent in each number?
- What does the 2 represent?
- What does the zero represent?
- How do you know which is the biggest number?

Now move on to further questions, such as:

- Using the same four digits, can you make a number between 4 025 and 4 205?
- Can you make a number smaller than 2 000? (e.g. 0 425)

Now put the following digits on the board:

3, 2, 4, 0

and ask the children to record on their individual whiteboards numbers such as:

- the largest four-digit number they can make
- the smallest four-digit number they can make
- a number between 2 030 and 3 000
- two numbers with four hundreds and three units

Summarise that we have been using our knowledge and understanding of place value to carry out this activity. We know that the value of a digit depends on where it is positioned and by moving digits around we can change numbers. We have been able to create different numbers using the same digits.

Simplify

For children who are not confident with four-digit numbers, ask them to engage in similar activities but with three-digit numbers.

Timing	Main
35 minutes	Explain that, although the number system we use today has been used for a long time, in the past the way we recorded numbers looked very different. Tell the children that during the lesson they are going to explore the system the Romans used to record numbers and at the end of the lesson you would like them to think about what is the same and what is different about the Roman system compared with the system we use today. Show the children the symbols the Romans used for 1 (I), 5 (V), 10 (X), 50 (L) and 100 (C). Now show them the following numbers written in Roman numerals and ask them to work in pairs to try and work out what numbers they might represent: • III, VIII, XVI, XXX, XXVII, LI

Take some responses, asking the children to justify their suggestions, but at this stage don't discount suggestions that don't follow the 'rules' the Romans devised. Explain that all number systems have been created over time and that to avoid confusion we all need to follow the same rules.

The Roman system created numbers by adding together the value of the numerals and recorded these using the fewest numerals possible; therefore XVI would be 10 + 5 + 1 =16. They nearly always recorded the biggest numerals they needed on the left and the smallest on the right. In pairs ask them to have a go at writing the following numbers using Roman numerals:

- 2, 7, 13, 28, 32, 83

Share their solutions and discuss any differences of opinion.

Now write the following on the board:

- IV and VI, IX and XI, XIV and XVI, XIX and XXI

With their partner ask them to discuss what is the same and what is different about each pair of numbers and what different numbers each set of numerals could represent. Take feedback and let the children share their ideas.

Now explain the next rule the Romans used. To prevent very long numbers, one smaller numeral could be used to the left of a larger numeral to show that this number was subtracted from the total — therefore instead of writing 4 as IIII you could write it as IV (5 − 1) and instead of writing 9 as VIIII you could write IX (10 − 1). Look back at the set of numbers on the board and clarify what numbers are represented by each set of numerals.

Ask the children to work in pairs to think how they would use this system to record:

- 14, 19, 24, 29, 34, 39

Take feedback.

Explain that as a class they are going to record all of the numbers from 1 to 100 as Roman numerals. Split the class into groups so that different groups are responsible for writing different numbers, e.g. 1–20, 21–40, 41–60, 61–80 and 81–100. In pairs the children need to agree how to record these numbers. They then compare their answers with another pair and where there is a difference of opinion they justify their reasoning. When the group has agreed their numbers they need to record their agreed numerals on the big piece of sugar paper (see Figure 9.1 on page 86).

Simplify

Give children the Roman numerals from 1 to 20 on pieces of card and the children could work in pairs to sort these into the correct order before copying them on to the large piece of sugar paper.

	Extend
	Challenge the children to write Roman numerals in response to questions such as:
	• How would you record 444 and 999?
	• How might you record 1 000? Justify your answer.
	• Start at 4 and count on in tens. Record this number pattern using Roman numerals. What patterns can you see in the way the numbers are recorded?
Timing	**Plenary/conclusion**
10 minutes	Record the following on the board and ask the children to discuss in pairs what is wrong with each of these and then to correct your mistakes:
	IIIIII, IIIX, VIX, XXXXX, XXXXXIIIIIIIII
	Take feedback.
	Now collect the large pieces of sugar paper and stick them together to make one large hundred square containing Roman numerals. Compare this hundred square to the one we use today. Ask questions such as:
	• What patterns can we see in our hundred square? Are there the same patterns in the Roman hundred square?
	• How many one-digit numbers are in our hundred square? Why is this different in the Roman hundred square?
	• How would the Romans have recorded 0? (They hadn't developed this symbol! Point out how important 0 is in our number system.)
	Help the children to recognise that the Romans used an additive system while we use a positional system (our place value system is built around the position/columns in which we place numbers).
	Over the next few days challenge the children to find examples of Roman numerals still being used today. Ask them to bring in images of these that can be shared with the class.

Assessment opportunities

This lesson involves regular opportunities for children to discuss their thinking in pairs. Listen to the language they use and their confidence in justifying their reasoning.

Whilst they are working, ask children questions such as these:

• Why have you decided to write the number that way?

• How do you know you've recorded it correctly? What rules did you use?

Commentary

Two particular features of this lesson include:

- asking children to justify their ideas and suggestions to develop their reasoning skills;
- using errors and misconceptions as a teaching tool.

Throughout the main part of the lesson there are regular opportunities for children to engage in paired discussion before being asked to explain their thinking to the whole class. It is important that children learn how to describe what they see and to explain their thinking as this helps to develop their reasoning skills. Discussion, in pairs, small groups or the whole class, provides children with different forums for practising how to explain their thinking and for getting feedback from peers or adults. It is important to give the children the opportunity to talk in pairs and small groups before expecting quality discussion as a whole group. Askew (2012) identifies the importance of both private talk and public conversation in mathematics. He refers to the talk and discussion that take place in pairs or as small groups as private talk as this enables children to share their ideas, rehearse their explanations and develop a shared understanding in a secure environment before engaging in a public conversation with the whole class.

Within the plenary children are invited to correct some mistakes made by the teacher. Hansen (2011) suggests that actively discussing potential errors and misconceptions with children can challenge them in their thinking and help them to reflect on their own learning. While making mistakes and gaining misconceptions are natural parts of learning and conceptual development, it can take time to develop a classroom ethos in which children are happy to share their own misunderstandings. Using mistakes made by the teacher or by an unknown child can be used as an alternative approach until children are happy to share mistakes they have made with a wider audience. Spooner (2002) suggests that correcting someone else's mistakes places the children in the role of the teacher and this can lead to a more open dialogue about the mistake which can then consolidate a child's own understanding.

Potential challenges

The numbers the children will find most challenging are those that involve the element of subtraction, e.g. 4, 9, 14, 19. Children may forget about this rule or apply the rule incorrectly; for example, they might record 19 as XVIIII or think they can record a number such as 8 as IIX (10 – 2). You might want to record a list of the 'tricky' numbers on the board to help remind the children of the numbers they can apply the subtraction rule to.

Look out for children who have a limited understanding of place value. Comparing and contrasting the Roman numerals to our number system may expose some gaps in understanding about how our number system works. Children may not have fully understood the significance of zero and how this is used as a place holder within our number system.

Ways the lesson could be adapted

For classes who find it challenging to work collaboratively the lesson could be structured so that children work in pairs to record as many numbers, using Roman numerals, as they can on a blank hundred square. They could then bring this to the plenary to compare and contrast it with our Hindu–Arabic hundred square.

For children who already have some prior knowledge of Roman numerals you could ask them to convert a number pattern into Roman numerals to explore whether similar patterns exist, e.g. 3, 13, 23, 33, 43, 53, etc. or 9, 18, 27, 36, 45, etc. This would again provide a good forum to compare and contrast the systems and to reinforce the importance of place value within the number system we use today.

How the learning might be developed in future lessons

Children could be challenged to solve some simple calculations using Roman numerals. The purpose of this would be to help reinforce how important our place value system is for calculating efficiently.

Exploring different number systems can help children to understand more fully the structure of the number system that they use.

- To explore another number system used by an ancient civilisation you could look at the ancient Egyptian numerals and how these combined to record numbers.

- You can also explore the ways that different cultures record numbers today. For example, you could look at how the Chinese script is recorded or how Bengali numbers are recorded. A simple idea is to use a hundred square that uses a script that is unknown to the children and cut this up into pieces like a jigsaw. The children then need to try and recreate the hundred square using the pattern of the symbols.

Key self-evaluation questions to help reflection on practice

- Do I regularly include opportunities for children to explain their thinking with a partner before exploring this with the whole class?

- Do I ask children to justify their choices and decisions in order to develop their reasoning skills?

- Do I highlight common errors and misconceptions to children and use these as a teaching tool?

- Do I regularly emphasise place value during my lessons to help children to understand how our number system works?

Further reading

Haylock, D. (2010) *Mathematics Explained*. (Chapter 6 – Number and place value.) London: Sage.

References

Askew, M. (2012) *Transforming Primary Mathematics*. London: Routledge.

DfE (2013) *The National Curriculum in England Key Stages 1 and 2 Framework Document.* London: Department for Education.

Hansen, I. (2011) *Children's Errors in Mathematics*. Exeter: Learning Matters.

Spooner, M. (2002) *Errors and Misconceptions in Maths at Key Stage 2: Working Towards Successful SATS.* London: David Fulton Publishers.

Chapter 10

Year 5: Big numbers

Learning outcomes

This chapter will help you to:

- appreciate that identifying given numbers, reading numbers out loud and writing them in numeral and written form are all important aspects of children's learning about number;
- realise the significance of children talking about the numbers they are working with;
- be aware of some of the difficulties associated with saying and writing large numbers;
- provide opportunities for children to see patterns within the base ten number system.

Reference to the Teachers' Standards

Working through this chapter will help you meet the following standards:

2. Promote good progress and outcomes by pupils.
3. Demonstrate good subject and curriculum knowledge.
4. Plan and teach well-structured lessons.
5. Adapt teaching to respond to the strengths and needs of all pupils.
6. Make accurate and productive use of assessment.

Links to the National Curriculum (DfE, 2013)

Year 5 programme of study (statutory requirements)

Pupils should be taught to:

- read, write, order and compare numbers to at least 1 000 000 and determine the value of each digit.

Notes and guidance (non-statutory)

Pupils identify the place value in large whole numbers.

Introduction

Many children find large numbers fascinating and will have met them in different contexts from an early age without necessarily knowing what numbers they are but being aware that they are large. They might have seen and noticed them on television, in car showrooms, at football matches, in newspapers, and so on. Children learn to work with increasingly large numbers as they progress through Key Stages 1 and 2. It is important that they have a secure understanding and knowledge of numbers and the value of the constituent digits as they progress. We would like them to know that, for example, 43 523 is 40 000 and 3 000 and 500 and 20 and 3, or 40 000 + 3 000 + 500 + 20 + 3 as well as know that if 40 000, 3 000, 500, 20 and 3 are combined, then we get 43 523. We would want children to be able to partition the number in other ways and know that 43 523 is closer to 44 000 than it is to 43 000. We need to encourage children to talk about the numbers they are working with, not simply deconstruct them mechanically. Saying the numbers is an important integral part of their learning – it can help children to become familiar with the patterns and structures as well as strengthen 'ownership'. Everyone owns numbers; they are not the property of the teacher, the textbook or worksheet, the curriculum or the test regime. Children love to create their own large numbers and the process of saying them and writing them down and/or dictating them for someone else to write down is a worthwhile activity in itself. The lesson in this chapter is planned to help children make sense of our number system and how it is used with large numbers. There is a strong focus on identifying pattern and structure and using these to construct large numbers. There are many ways in which children can be encouraged to engage with large numbers from the world around them, and some ideas are provided in the section on 'How the learning might be developed in future lessons', but the emphases for the lesson are on combining and partitioning large numbers, reading, saying and recording numbers.

If you have not already done so, you may want to read the introduction to the Year 2 lesson plan on place value in Chapter 2; much of the information provided is also relevant to this chapter.

Lesson plan

Year 5: Big numbers	
Focused learning objectives	**Success criteria**
Starter: Recognise, read and write sequences of numbers being multiplied by ten each time **Main:** Recognise the value of each digit in numbers up to a million Read and write numbers up to a million	Be able to partition numbers with up to six digits Know the value of each digit with numbers up to six digits Read numbers with up to six digits Write numbers with up to six digits

Vocabulary

hundred thousand, million, place value chart

Resources

Starter

- Individual whiteboards and pens

Main

- Place value chart (Figure 10.1) with rows from millions through to units/ones – ideally an electronic version that can be annotated for the whole class to see

1 000 000	2 000 000	3 000 000	4 000 000	5 000 000	6 000 000	7 000 000	8 000 000	9 000 000
100 000	200 000	300 000	400 000	500 000	600 000	700 000	800 000	900 000
10 000	20 000	30 000	40 000	50 000	60 000	70 000	80 000	90 000
1 000	2 000	3 000	4 000	5 000	6 000	7 000	8 000	9 000
100	200	300	400	500	600	700	800	900
10	20	30	40	50	60	70	80	90
1	2	3	4	5	6	7	8	9

Figure 10.1 Place value chart

- Sets of place value charts for pupils to use (ideally laminated so that they can be written on)
- Sets of prepared number cards, reflecting differing needs. For example, one set might include numbers over a million, another set might be numbers up to a million and one set might consist of numbers up to ten thousand. You will need enough sets so that there is one set between two children (approximately ten cards in each set)
- Individual whiteboards and pens

Timing	Starter/introduction
10/15 minutes	Write the following numbers on the board, making sure that the digits are aligned to represent their value. Explain that you would like children to watch you and think about what you are doing.

Write:

3

30

300

Now ask the children what number you might write next, asking them to talk to their partner and agree how it would be written and read. Establish that 3 000 is the number written in numerals and three thousand is how we read it. Ask how they knew this was the next number. From the feedback given, establish that it is ten times bigger than the previous number (they may describe how the digit 3 moves into the next column or has an extra zero to show the number is bigger). Record 3 000 on the board. Continue with thirty thousand and three hundred thousand, being aware that some children may become less confident as the numbers increase. Emphasise the 'thirty' in thirty thousand, and 'three hundred' in three hundred thousand, as these are the parts of numbers some children find difficult to read. The recording on the board should help reinforce the position of the digits and the written form.

Now ask for the next number (three million) and go through the process as above. Now ask the children to read, with you, the numbers you have written down on the board. As the children read the numbers, write the number in words alongside each number on the board.

Now ask children to work in pairs and choose a different single-digit number and then take their number up to millions, recording on a whiteboard the different stages and making sure they can read each number. Take some feedback, asking a few children to read out their set of numbers to the rest of the class.

Support

Prepare a set of cards, e.g. 5, 50, 500, 5 000, 50 000, 500 000, 5 000 000, and a set of cards with the corresponding written forms. Shuffle the cards and ask children to put the number cards in order and then match up to the cards with numbers in written form and ask children to read the numbers.

Ask children to choose their own start number (between 0 and 10) and create their own set of numbers, using the card set they have to support their thinking.

Challenge

Ask children to start with a two-digit number and carry out the task as above. See how far they can take their number, being clear they can read it and say it, write it in numerals and in words. Alternatively, ask

<table>
<tr><td></td><td>children to start with a number such as 403 and continue to make it ten times bigger for as long as they can! Again, it is important for children to be able to read and say their numbers. Children could then be asked to choose their own start number.</td></tr>
<tr><td>Timing

30 minutes</td><td>**Main**

Show the place value chart (see Figure 10.1 on page 95) and ask children to talk to the person next to them about what they can see and what they notice. Ask them to think of three things each. Take feedback and establish that the numbers in the rows are increasing from ones/units to millions. Point to a number and ask someone to read the number being pointed to. Repeat for different numbers.

Now model combining numbers, e.g. underline/circle 2 000, 900, 30, 7 and explain that if we combine these numbers our combined number would be two thousand, nine hundred and thirty-seven. Point to each component part as it is read and write it as 2 937.

Now circle several numbers in different rows, reading them as you do so, e.g. circle 6 000, 500, 70, 4. Ask the children to discuss with a partner and agree how to say and write the number that is obtained when these parts are put together. Repeat several times, going up to tens of thousands and then hundreds of thousands. Note that using tens of thousands and hundreds of thousands gets tricky because you cannot simply read the component parts; you have to wait to see what follows. For example, if you circle 300 000 and then 70 000, you need to know both numbers before you can put them together to give three hundred and seventy thousand. It will therefore be easier to let the children know all the numbers before they try to combine the different parts. Establish how the numbers are said and how they are written, in numerals and in words. Children could be asked to record these numbers on their whiteboards. Do allow time for children to discuss these numbers before asking them to record the numbers (in numerals and in words) on their whiteboards.

Now write down a number (e.g. 54 923) and ask children which numbers on the chart would need to be circled to create the number you have written. Again, ask them to discuss with a partner and perhaps record on their whiteboards. Repeat this several times, making sure that at least one of the numbers modelled contains zero. e.g. 603 567.

Explain that children are now going to be number detectives and find the parts that make up a number.

Model the activity as follows. Using a set of cards (maybe those up to a million) ask a child to choose one of the cards. Show it to the class. Can they say the number to their partner? When all are agreed, draw attention</td></tr>
</table>

to the place value chart. Now, can they discuss with their partner which numbers would need to be circled to combine together to create the number on the card? Ask children to feed back and instruct you to circle the numbers – encourage them to be clear in their instructions and ask them to give you them in order of size, one number for each digit. Carry out their instructions and then ask if this is correct. Try to avoid making any judgement at this stage; you want the children to tell you whether the correct numbers have been circled. When all agree, explain that they are going to do this activity in pairs, using different sets of cards.

Set up the activity in pairs so that one person chooses a card and reads it out to the partner. When the partner agrees it has been read correctly they circle the numbers needed for each digit and when both children agree this is correct, they record the number, e.g. 57 302, and write down the numbers they circled, e.g. 50 000, 7 000, 300, 2. Emphasise that they must read out the number on the card before finding the numbers on the grid. When they have done this, children can write down the number in words.

Support

Use cards with fewer digits.

Challenge

Use cards with numbers up to and beyond a million.

An extension for all groups is to write their own numbers for their partner and carry out the activity as above.

Timing	Plenary/conclusion
10 minutes	<ul><li>Ask pairs to talk about which numbers they found easy and which numbers they found difficult. Take feedback and then provide some additional numbers for them to consider. For example, 7 000, 50 032, 7 824, 97 378, 124 048. Write them on the board for all to see and ask them, without circling numbers on their charts, how they would say those numbers. Are they easy? Are they difficult? Why?</li><li>Ask children if they can go away and find some big numbers – in newspapers, on television, on their computers – and bring them into school. Can we find some numbers less than a million but bigger than ten thousand?</li></ul>

Assessment opportunities

Whilst they are working, ask children questions such as these. You might want to focus on those children whose level of understanding you are unsure about. These might be children you think are unclear or children whose thinking you can extend.

- Can you explain to me why you've circled those numbers on the chart?
- What number would be one more/ten more/hundred more than the number on your card?
- What number would you get if you circled 400 instead of 300 on your chart?
- Can you think of a number that would only need two numbers to be circled on the chart? What about a number with six digits that only needs two numbers to be circled?

Commentary

This lesson aims to strengthen children's understanding of place value/ digit value with larger numbers and provides an opportunity for them to read and write large numbers. By using the place value chart (also known as Gattegno chart, named after Caleb Gattegno, a French mathematics educator), children can visualise the constituent parts of a number. The chart can be an effective tool in helping children to appreciate the patterns in our counting structure. Children should have some familiarity with the layout and ways in which it can be used before carrying out the lesson described.

Potential challenges

Children sometimes experience difficulty in reading and saying large numbers. Generally, they are confident with numbers up to four digits because the number (3 965, for example) can be read as three thousand, nine hundred and sixty-five, and this emphasises the individual digit values. However, beyond thousands, digits have to be interpreted as tens of thousands, hundreds of thousands and then millions, and the process becomes less straightforward. With large numbers the digits are grouped in threes and this pattern can be explored with children (Aduba et al., 1997). First there are ones, tens and hundreds. Then, there are thousands, tens of thousands and hundreds of thousands. The next group of three is millions, tens of millions and hundreds of millions.

A zero in the number can also cause difficulties so we need to make sure children have the opportunity to see numbers containing zero represented on the place value chart to demonstrate that we may not need a number in every row on the chart. When asked to record numbers containing zero, some children will struggle with larger numbers. They may be confident and accurate with numbers such as four thousand and sixty-two, recognising in the spoken or written form that there are no hundreds. However, a number such as seventy thousand, nine hundred and twenty-four provides no such clues. Using place value cards (see Figure 10.2) and collecting and positioning 70 000, 900, 20 and 4 will help children to see how the number is written.

The ways in which large numbers are written in numerals needs consideration. Throughout this chapter a space has been used to signal a 'break' in the number for easier reading. Many textbooks and published materials use this, although there are still occasions when a comma is used to break up numbers (e.g. 51,234 or 51 234). The convention is to include a break or comma to distinguish thousands then millions then thousands of millions, and so on. However, this is not always used and sometimes we see no break separating thousands from hundreds (e.g. 4518).

Ways the lesson could be adapted

- Other equipment could be used. For example, an extended set of place value cards could be used where cards using thousands or tens of thousands, or even hundreds of thousands are created. For children who find it difficult to partition, for example, 49 000 into 40 000 and 9 000, and read out these constituent parts, place value cards can be particularly helpful (Figure 10.2).

40 000   9 000

Figure 10.2 Place value cards

- There are various calculator activities that can be used to support these ideas and offer another way of recording numbers. The sets of cards described for the main part of the lesson could be used and children take it in turn to read out a number (without their partner seeing the card) and their partner has to tap the number into the calculator. Once this has been done, both children can check to see if the number on the card matches the one in the calculator. This requires good listening skills, but the number read out can be repeated as many times as you allow. When all the cards have been used, the two children can put them in order.

- Another activity using a calculator goes by the name of Place Invaders! There are various versions of this paired activity but one version is as follows:

  o One child enters a five-digit number (or any number of digits as is appropriate).

  o Their partner has to 'shoot down' the digits so that the calculator eventually shows 0 in the display. The aim is to do this in as few 'shots' as possible.

  Each shot involves:

  − using the $\boxed{-}$ key

  − using the $\boxed{0}$ key as many times as the child likes

  − using only one other digit key.

  For example, child A enters 96 723 into the calculator.

  Child B presses $\boxed{-}\boxed{6}\boxed{0}\boxed{0}\boxed{0}\boxed{=}$

  and calculator shows 90 723.

  Child B has managed to 'shoot' down the 7 digit and has had one shot.

  Child B continues to take shots and tries to do so in as few shots as possible.

  o Change over roles.

  Children can carry out this activity several times. You might like to make it a rule of the game that the one changing digits to zero has to explain to the partner what he or she is going to do and predict what the new number might be before making the key presses.

- The activity in the main part of the lesson could be followed up using a place value grid (Figures 10.3 and 10.4) or a spike abacus (Figure 10.5). This changes the

100 000s	10 000s	1 000s	100s	10s	1s

Figure 10.3 Place value grid (numbers)

Hundreds of thousands	Tens of thousands	Thousands	Hundreds	Tens	Ones

Figure 10.4 Place value grid (words)

nature of the activity because the partitioning and combining do not occur but the value of digits is demonstrated in a different way. Numbers can be recorded using these structures and can be read and written in words, for example.

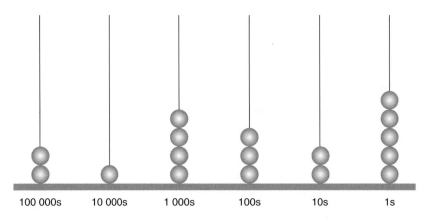

        100 000s   10 000s   1 000s   100s   10s   1s

Figure 10.5 Spike abacus representing 214 325

How the learning might be developed in future lessons

Children can use digit cards (two sets of 0–9 cards shuffled and placed face down) to create their own multi-digit numbers. For example, two children, each using their own place value grid as above, take turns to take a digit card and place on their grid wherever they choose. They continue to do this until their place value grid is full. They then each read out their number and maybe write it down in words.

This activity could be made into a game by aiming for:

- the number closest to a million or

- the smallest number or

- the number closest to half a million, and so on.

The activity using the place value chart at the beginning of the lesson can be used slightly differently. Instead of pointing to and circling numbers on the chart in order of magnitude, vary the order. So, for example, you may point to 700 then 20 000 then

40 then 5 then 9 000 without circling and ask the children to write down the numbers as you point to them. Children could then be asked to decide what number is obtained when these parts are put together. This provides further opportunity for children to think about constituent parts of a number and how they are combined.

Try to include the use of real-life situations where large numbers occur. For example, collect and order attendance figures for football matches, lottery wins, house prices, and so on. Make a poster or display showing these figures with their context, maybe from newspaper cuttings. Pose questions such as: which is the largest number? or which number is closest to one hundred thousand? Make use of numbers written as numerals and written as words.

Children can be set a whole variety of challenges to bring to life large numbers. Can children collect/find large numbers of something (centimetre squares, seeds, dots, printed words)? What might cost £1 000 000? How far would a million 1p pieces stretch? Have we been alive for a million seconds? A million minutes? How high would a pile of a million pieces of paper be?

Key self-evaluation questions to help reflection on practice

- Am I clear about how various images and materials offer different representations of large numbers?

- Do I emphasise the use of reading out loud numbers as well as writing them?

- Do I regularly model to the children how the mathematics can be recorded?

- Do I plan a range of probing questions I can ask during mathematics lessons to help me to assess the depth of children's understanding?

- Do I develop children's understanding of number by encouraging them to visualise numbers in their heads?

- Do I encourage children to talk about the numbers they are working with?

Further reading

Cotton, T. (2013) *Understanding and Teaching Primary Mathematics*. (Chapter 4 – Counting and understanding number.) Harlow: Pearson.

References

Aduba, N., Drabble, S., Hafeez, R. et al. (1997) *Starting from Mathematical Ideas: Big Numbers*. London: BEAM (no longer in print).

DfE (2013) *The National Curriculum in England Key Stages 1 and 2 Framework Document*. London: Department for Education.

Chapter 11

Year 6: Understanding decimals

Learning outcomes

This chapter will help you to:

- understand the need to reinforce place value when helping children understand decimal numbers;
- recognise the importance of using the language of tenths, hundredths and thousandths when referring to the digits after the decimal point;
- have a greater understanding of some of the potential challenges children may face when using decimal numbers.

Reference to the Teachers' Standards

Working through this chapter will help you meet the following standards:

3. Demonstrate good subject and curriculum knowledge.
4. Plan and teach well-structured lessons.
5. Adapt teaching to respond to the strengths and needs of all pupils.
6. Make accurate and productive use of assessment.

Links to the National Curriculum (DfE, 2013)

Year 6 programme of study (statutory requirements)

Pupils should be taught to:

- identify the value of each digit in numbers given to three decimal places.

Introduction

Decimal numbers extend our place value system to include fractional parts of a number. Therefore a very good understanding of our place value system when using whole numbers is important in order for children to understand decimals. As with whole numbers, the value of each digit depends upon its position within the number, with the decimal point being used to separate the whole amounts from the parts of the whole. When using decimal notation with children it is therefore important to continue using the language of place value to help them understand the value of each digit and appreciate the size of the number. However because of the way we read the numbers after the decimal point, this is not always easy. When reading a whole number such as 145 we would say 'one hundred and forty-five' and so make some reference to the size of each digit. However when reading a number such as 1.45 we would typically say 'one point four five'. This makes no reference at all to the language of tenths and hundredths, and so does little to reinforce to children the value of each digit. Alternatively children may read it as 'one point forty-five' (possibly linking it to how we would read an amount of money such as £1.45) without realising that in this case the 'forty-five' is actually forty-five hundredths. It is therefore important that children understand and are able to refer to this number as one unit, four tenths and five hundredths. To reinforce this language it is useful to make links to fractions as this decimal representation is based on the fractions $\frac{1}{10}$, $\frac{1}{100}$, $\frac{1}{1000}$, etc.

Consequently 1.45 is one unit, $\frac{4}{10}$ and $\frac{5}{100}$ or one unit and $\frac{45}{100}$

To help children to understand decimal notation it may be necessary to assess their understanding of place value of whole numbers quickly before introducing tenths, hundredths and then thousandths. The programmes of study in the 2013 National Curriculum for Year 3 children include *count up and down in tenths; recognise that tenths arise from dividing an object into 10 equal parts and in dividing one-digit numbers or quantities by 10* and for Year 4 children to *count up and down in hundredths; recognise that hundredths arise when dividing an object by one hundred and dividing tenths by ten* (DfE, 2013).

Lesson plan

Year 6: Understanding decimals	
Focused learning objectives	**Success criteria**
Starter: solve problems involving the size of numbers **Main:** identify the value of each digit in numbers to three decimal places	Know that the numbers after the decimal point are tenths, hundredths and thousandths Use the value of digits in numbers to three decimal places to identify the relative size of a number

Vocabulary

place value, digit, ones, units, tenths, hundredths, thousandths, decimal, decimal point, decimal place, descending

Resources

Starter

- Children may want individual whiteboards and pens to record their thinking on

Main

- Place value apparatus to provide visual support as necessary (see the models, images and resources suggested later in this chapter)

- Sets of cards with the following or similar statements on them if the game suggested in the extension is used.

  o The biggest number possible

  o The smallest number possible

  o A number bigger than 5.4

  o A number with 5 thousandths

  o A number smaller than 2.3

Timing	Starter/introduction
10/15 minutes	Explain that you are going to give the class some statements about numbers. In pairs they need to decide if each statement is: - always true - sometimes true - never true They will need to provide examples and convincing reasons for their decision and be prepared to share their answer and their reasoning with the whole class. 1. The more digits a number has, then the larger its value 2. A number with two decimal places is bigger than a number with one decimal place

3. A number that has a decimal point is smaller than a number that doesn't

Take feedback, dealing with any differences of opinion and question the children to ensure they are clear about when the statement is true and when it is not true.

Support: Ask questions to support children with their reasoning. For example ask children if they can write numbers to show that the statement is true. Then ask if they can think of any numbers that would show that the statement isn't true.

Timing	Main
30 minutes	Record a number with three decimal places on the board, e.g. 44.444, and ask the children to read the number out loud. Now ask them what each of the digits is worth. Record it on a place value grid (Figure 11.1) to emphasise the value of each digit, particularly those after the decimal point. Explain that in the lesson you want them to use the language of tenths, hundredths and thousandths when reading decimal numbers.

H	T	U	●	t	h	th
	4	4	●	4	4	4

Figure 11.1 Decimal place value grid

Ask questions to assess their understanding and to check that they understand how 0 is used as a place holder. For example, record the number 44.044 and ask the children to discuss with a partner whether they think this is a bigger or smaller number than 44.444 and why. How about 44.440? Why can we also write 44.440 as 44.44? How about 44.404? Can we also write this as 44.44? Why/Why not?

Record some of the above on the place value chart to reinforce the value of each digit.

Now record a range of different pairs of numbers on the board, such as:

   97.8 and 9.87   9.78 and 9.68   9.87 and 9.867

   9.678 and 9.867   968.7 and 9.687

Check that the children can identify what the digit 8 is worth in each of these numbers.

Then ask children firstly to convince their partner and then be ready to convince you which is the bigger number in each pair. Discuss their responses and ask questions such as:

- How did you decide which number was bigger?
- Which pair of numbers was the trickiest? Why?

	Now write four digits on the board, for example, 5 3 4 2. Explain that you want them to use these digits to make a number with three decimal places (□.□□□), for example, 5.342. Challenge them to make:
	• the biggest number possible
	• the smallest number possible
	• a number bigger than 5.4
	• a number with 5 thousandths
	• a number smaller than 2.3 (why isn't this possible if you use all four numbers?)
	Discuss their responses.
	Explain that you are going to give the children other sets of digits and with each set you would like them to make numbers that have three decimal places that fit the same categories you've just used. If it isn't possible to make one of the numbers they should state why.
	The sets of digits could include 1 5 2 8, 1 7 3 5, 2 3 5 3, 1 5 1 5, 3 0 5 5, 2 4 0 5, 3 0 0 5.
	Simplify
	Adapt the activity to focus on numbers with one or two decimal places (for example, give sets of three digits to make □.□□ or □□.□).
	Provide the children with a structured resource such as place value apparatus (see the models, images and resources suggested later in this chapter) to help them to visualise the size of the numbers.
	Extension
	Provide children with sets with more digits to enable them to make □□.□□□ or □.□□□□ numbers, for example:
	1 2 3 4 5, 5 3 0 4 0 2
	Alternatively the activity could be developed into a game by printing copies of the categories on to cards, shuffling them and placing them face down on the table. In pairs each of the children could be challenged to make a number with three decimal places. They then select a category card and if the number they have created fulfils the category, they win a point. The first to reach 5 points wins.
Timing 10 minutes	**Plenary/conclusion** Record the following pairs of numbers on the board and ask the children to identify which number in each pair is the bigger number and why: • 1.516 and 1.651 • 5.053 and 5.503 • 0.165 and 0.17

- 0.2 and 0.10
- 0.650 and 0.65

Now write these numbers on the board and challenge the children to write them in ascending order.

1.023   1.03   1.320   1.302   1.3

Finally ask the children to work in pairs to suggest some useful tips they could give each other in order to know which number in a pair of decimal numbers is the bigger.

Assessment opportunities

During the whole-class teaching input and while the children are working, listen for accurate use of place value language such as tenths, hundredths and thousandths.

While the children are working ask questions to assess their understanding, such as:

- How do you know that this number is bigger than this number?
- What does this digit stand for? How do you know?

Commentary

The starter for the lesson uses 'sometimes, always, never true' statements as an opportunity for children to discuss their thinking with a partner to prepare them for justifying their reasoning as part of a whole-class discussion. This type of activity encourages children to produce examples and counterexamples to test whether a statement is true or not. Haylock (2010) discusses the key processes in mathematical reasoning and highlights the importance of engaging children in generalisations and encouraging them to consider possible counterexamples and special cases. Swan (2005) supports using statements such as these as they potentially provide the opportunity to expose children to cognitive conflict by exploring their existing beliefs and any possible contradictions. They can be used by a teacher as a mechanism to confront common misconceptions and as a vehicle to help children develop their ability to explain their thinking with conviction. The teacher therefore has an important role during such discussions to challenge learners to think deeply and develop convincing reasons.

Within the main part of the lesson children continue to be challenged by being asked to consider whether some of the numbers they are being asked to generate are possible (e.g. can they make a number smaller than 2.3 with the digits they have been given?). This again puts them in the position of explaining why but also challenges the perceptions of some children, who may believe that mathematics is always about finding the 'right answer'.

Potential challenges

There are a number of common misconceptions when using decimal numbers and it is important to include examples that will help to highlight and expose these. Common difficulties can include:

- the pronunciation of decimal numbers. Children can easily mishear tenths, hundredths and thousandths as tens, hundreds and thousands, so it is important that adults and children pronounce these clearly;

- assuming that the number with more digits must be the larger number, e.g. some children will assume that 2.125 is bigger than 2.2 (some children may read this as two point one hundred and twenty-five, and this sounds much larger than two point two);

- assuming that the more digits, the smaller the number. This may be because for whole numbers they have learnt that the more digits, the larger the number so therefore assume that with decimal numbers the opposite is true;

- insecure knowledge of place value can also cause difficulties when comparing numbers with a different number of decimal places, e.g. 1.4 and 1.21.

Ways the lesson could be adapted

The context of measurement could have been used throughout the lesson. Since there are 1000 grams in a kilogram and 1000 millilitres in a litre, the lesson could be put in the context of either mass or capacity. Contexts can give the children confidence in dealing with decimal notation as they present the mathematics in a less abstract and more familiar setting. For example, they could consider pairs of numbers such as 1.516 and 1.651 in the context of which is heavier – 1.516 kg or 1.651 kg?

To help children develop a broad and deep understanding of place value you could also integrate a range of resources, models and images into the lesson. Some of the structured resources, models and images you might use to help children appreciate the size of the digits in decimal numbers include place value apparatus (Figure 11.2), decimal place value cards (Figure 11.3), place value charts (Figure 11.4) and number lines (Figure 11.5).

Figure 11.2   Place value apparatus

Use place value apparatus to represent decimal numbers. If the 'flat' represents one whole, then the 'stick' represents a tenth and the single cube represents one-hundredth. So, Figure 11.2 represents one whole, one tenth and four hundredths (1.14).

Figure 11.3   Decimal place value cards

How the learning might be developed in future lessons

Number lines provide a powerful image for helping children with the position of a number in relation to other numbers. Locating and positioning numbers on a number line require a good understanding of place value and of the relative size of numbers.

1 000	2 000	3 000	4 000	5 000	6 000	7 000	8 000	9 000
100	200	300	400	500	600	700	800	900
10	20	30	40	50	60	70	80	90
1	2	3	4	5	6	7	8	9
0.1	0.2	0.3	0.4	0.5	0.6	0.7	0.8	0.9
0.01	0.02	0.03	0.04	0.05	0.06	0.07	0.08	0.09
0.001	0.002	0.003	0.004	0.005	0.006	0.007	0.008	0.009

Figure 11.4   Place value charts

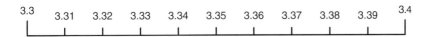

Figure 11.5   Number lines

Within the context of identifying the value of each digit in numbers given to three decimal places, the National Curriculum (DfE, 2013) also suggests that children multiply and divide numbers by 10, 100 and 1 000, giving answers up to three decimal places. When multiplying by 10 it is important that children understand that the digits all move one place to the left (two places for 100 and three places for 1 000), whereas when dividing by 10 they move one place to the right (or two for 100 and three for 1 000). A common misconception is that when multiplying by 10 you simply add a 0. Unfortunately this only works for some numbers and causes difficulties when applied to decimals, e.g. adding a zero to 2.71 gives you 2.710, which is exactly the same number. Alternatively another misconception related to 'add a 0' might be to put the 0 after the units digit, and as a result children may think 2.71 multiplied by 10 is 20.71. However by moving the digits one place to the left, $2.71 \times 10 = 27.1$.

Key self-evaluation questions to help reflection on practice

- Do I regularly make reference to the language of tenths, hundredths and thousandths when referring to the digits after the decimal point?

- Do I help develop children's reasoning skills by asking them to justify whether a statement is sometimes, always or never true?

- Do I sometimes challenge the thinking of children by presenting them with questions that cannot be answered?

References

DfE (2013) *The National Curriculum in England Key Stages 1 and 2 Framework Document.* London: Department for Education.

Haylock, D. (2010) *Mathematics Explained for Primary Teachers.* London, UK: Sage.

Swan, M. (2005) *Improving Learning in Mathematics: Challenges and Strategies.* London: DfES.

Chapter 12

Year 6: Reading scales

Learning outcomes

This chapter will help you to:

- identify a way of supporting children to develop skills in interpreting and reading scales;
- appreciate the role of teacher modelling in scaffolding children's learning;
- identify ways of providing opportunities for children to describe, discuss, explain and justify their ideas.

Reference to the Teachers' Standards

Working through this chapter will help you meet the following standards:

2. Promote good progress and outcomes by pupils.
3. Demonstrate good subject and curriculum knowledge.
4. Plan and teach well-structured lessons.

Links to the National Curriculum (DfE, 2013)

Although the programmes of study do not specifically refer to reading scales, it is a skill that is needed in various mathematics contexts, including aspects of measurement and statistics. The use of various measuring scales is referred to throughout Key Stages 1 and 2.

Introduction

Reading scales is an important skill when using measuring instruments and interpreting graphs and charts. Children can experience difficulties when reading scales, particularly when they need to interpret the value of intervals. This chapter provides a lesson plan which can be used to help children identify the process needed to interpret scale. This involves working out the 'value' of an interval and, subsequently, labelling unnumbered but marked points on the scale. The lesson begins with using scales within the context of units of measure and then moves on to using number-only scales, i.e. number lines. The process of interpretation is a key element of the activities.

Sometimes, children are expected to read scales simply by using trial and improvement strategies, or by answering step-by-step questions from the teacher. These approaches may enable children to answer specific questions but they do not always support them to develop generalisations. It is helpful if the process is explored and, to some extent, formalised with the children.

Lesson plan

Year 6: Reading scales	
Focused learning objectives	**Success criteria**
Starter Position numbers up to 1 000 on a number line *Main* Be able to write/give instructions for interpreting and reading a scale Read a variety of scales	Identify which numbers given on a scale/number line can be used to work out the scale being used Calculate the 'value' of intervals on a scale/number line Count on or back in appropriate steps Fill in missing numbers on a scale/number line

Vocabulary
interval, position, division

Resources
Starter • Number cards for children to position on an empty number line (for example, 0, 50, 200, 250, 300, 400, 450, 1 000). These need to be large enough for everyone to see *Main* • Images of scales (as described below in the main part of the lesson) • Weighing scales • Measuring jug • Number line scales for children to write on *Plenary* • Individual whiteboards and pens (one between two)

Timing	Starter/introduction
10/15 minutes	Explain that you are going to create a class number line. Ideally you will need plenty of space (this activity could be done outside) as it is good to develop your number line so that, as it is being built, everyone can see the numbers. Ask one child to stand at the beginning of what is going to be your number line, giving that child the number card with 0 on it. Now ask another child to stand at the other end of your number line, giving this child the number card 1 000. Now distribute the rest of the number cards (maybe one between two children) and ask them to remain where they are but to think about where they will position themselves between 0 and 1 000. Now start with the children holding number 200 and ask where they think this number should be placed and why. Make sure

children provide some reasoning; maybe they will tell you that it is one-fifth of the way between 0 and 1000, or that 100 would be one-tenth along the line, so 200 should be two-tenths. Continue to ask pairs to explain where they think their number should be positioned and why. A good order for the numbers to be added to the number line would be:

200, 50, 750, 300, 950, 500, 250, 400, 450, 650, 850

As each new number is added, involve other children in the discussion by asking them to discuss with their partner if they think the position is right and why. It is important that they are looking at the position of the numbers and not just whether they are in the right order. You may want to ask one child from each pair to bring out his or her number and stand in the number line, otherwise the number line can become crowded. Alternatively, you could ask one child in each pair to move towards the number line whilst the partner directs him or her.

Support

- Consider which numbers will be easier to position on the number line. Numbers such as 500, 250 and 750 will be easier (to justify and position) than numbers such as 850, for example.

Challenge

- Children can be challenged to give further justification for positioning/not positioning numbers. You could suggest an inappropriate position for a given number and ask children to convince you it should not be placed there.
- Mark a point somewhere beyond 1 000 – what number do they think would go there if the number line continued? Why?
- Where would 1 250 go? What about 1 500? What about 1 100? and so on.

Timing	Main
30 minutes	 0g 1 000g **Figure 12.1** Scale A Show a version of the scale in Figure 12.1 to the class. Ask the children to discuss in pairs what they notice about what they can see. Take feedback and establish that it is a scale and similar ones may be seen on weighing scales, usually curved. You may also want to consider the numbers the children can see and the range of numbers displayed. Have weighing scales for children to see. Ask when such scales might be used. Take feedback. Explain that in order to measure accurately we need to understand how the scale is set up and how we can interpret the markings.

Explain that you want to label each mark on the scale and you are going to think out loud as you do so to model your thinking. It may go something like this:

'This is the beginning of the scale and is 0g. This is the end of the scale and is 1 000g. I am going to count the intervals, one, two, three, four, five' (showing your counting as you do so). 'Each interval is equally spaced so has to be equal . . . five equal intervals from 0 to 1 000, so divide 1 000 by 5 . . . 200. Let me check by counting up in 200s'. (Count up in 200s and move along the scale as you do so, reaching 1 000g.) 'So each interval is 200g. So, I can label each marking. 0 is already marked, so 200g, 400g, 600g, 800g and then 1 000g are already marked'. Write in the correct numbers as you go along the scale.

Ask the children to imagine someone had just come into the room and they missed your 'out-loud thinking'. Then ask children, in pairs, to talk to each other, telling the story of what you did. Take some feedback for a 'retell'.

Explain that you are going to go through the same sort of process again, using a different scale (Figure 12.2).

Figure 12.2 Scale B

Show this to the class. Explain that, again, you want to label each mark on the scale and you are going to think out loud as you do so. This time, before you start the process, ask the children to think about what you might say and do. Ask them to share this with their partner.

Now talk your thinking out loud. It may go something like this:

'This is 300ml and this is 400ml. I am going to count the intervals, one, two, three, four' (showing your counting as you do so). 'Each interval is equally spaced so has to be equal . . . four intervals from 300 to 400. From 300ml to 400ml is a difference of 100ml, so there are four equal intervals for 100ml. So, divide 100 by 4 . . . 25. Let me check by counting up in 25s'. (Start at 300 and count up in 25s and move up the scale as you do so, reaching 400.) 'So each interval is 25ml. So, I can label each marking. 300ml is already marked, so 325ml, 350ml, 375ml, and then 400ml are already marked'. Write in the correct numbers as you go along the scale.

Again, ask the children to imagine someone had just come into the room and they missed your 'out-loud thinking'. Then ask children, in pairs, to talk to each other, telling the story of what you did. Take some feedback for a 'retell'.

Explain that you are now going to look at a number line where scale has been used (Figure 12.3).

360   380

Figure 12.3   Scale C

Show this to the class. Ask them to copy this on to their whiteboards (one between two). This will help them to look carefully at the numbers provided, the intervals and the relative positioning.

Now explain that you want them to use the same sort of thinking that was used earlier to try to

- work out the size of the intervals
- work out the numbers of all the points that are marked
- provide an explanation

Take feedback and ask someone to come out and put the missing numbers on the number line. Does everyone agree? Can they justify their numbering?

Support
- Support the paired discussions with prompting questions.

Challenge
- For the first two scenarios, ask children to identify numbers bigger or smaller than the range being looked at.
- For any of the scales used, ask children what numbers might be in the middle of marked intervals and ask them to justify their response.

Now provide children with number lines representing different scales, with only some of the points numbered. (Some examples of the types you might use are given in Figures 12.4–12.10.) Their task is to number the rest of the points. Ask them to do the first few in pairs, talking through the process. Then ask them to work individually on the next few but be prepared to share their thinking with their partner when finished. Make sure the number lines, when produced for the children, allow ample space for them to write in the numbers. You may wish to show them how to make best use of the space available when labelling the points.

For some of the scales you could ask where specific points might be placed. For example, on scale E (Figure 12.5), you could ask where the following numbers would be placed: 3 500, 500, 7 500.

The scales used can be varied according to the needs of the children; the ones given here provide a variety of levels of difficulty in interpretation and reading.

Figure 12.4   Scale D

Figure 12.5   Scale E

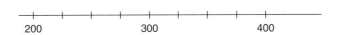

Figure 12.6   Scale F

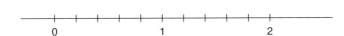

Figure 12.7   Scale G

Figure 12.8   Scale H

Figure 12.9   Scale I

Figure 12.10   Scale J

Timing	Plenary/conclusion
10 minutes	Look at some of the scales children have worked on. Ask children to talk through the process of finding the 'size' of the interval, counting up or down to check, and then labelling points on the number line.
	Ask children, in pairs, to discuss what they think are the key parts of the process. Ask them to 'say' the instructions, one at a time, to their partner and then, using their whiteboards, attempt to write down the instructions for someone else to follow.
	Follow up by asking one or more pairs to read through their instructions. If there is time, try it out with a new scale.

Assessment opportunities

Whilst they are working ask children a range of questions. You might want to focus on those children whose level of understanding you are unsure about. These might be children you think are unclear or children whose thinking you can extend.

You could ask questions such as:

- How did you know the intervals were going up in 50s?

- What would the next number on the scale be?

- How many intervals are there here? What's the difference in the two numbers? So how could we work out how much each interval is worth?

- Suppose someone said that they thought this point was the number 750. Do you think they could be right? Why/Why not?

- Can you explain each stage that you went through?

- What if someone wanted to know where 420 would be positioned on the scale – how could you work that out?

Commentary

The lesson aims to encourage children to think about how scales can be interpreted and, consequently, to work out any missing numbers or readings. It is a skill that some children find difficult; this lesson provides children with some scaffolding to develop the skill. Like many skills, it improves with practice, but has to be based on an understanding of what the process might involve. The lesson makes use of teacher modelling in the sense that the teacher is making his or her thinking explicit. This is intended to be used as an opportunity for the teacher to share thinking and for children to respond by interpreting the 'story' in relation to the context being used. This is different to a simple explanation of how a process is carried out with an expectation that children copy or imitate the process without thought.

The beginning of the main part of the lesson uses a real-life context of measurement to prompt thought and discussion about the interpretation of scale. The lesson then moves to more abstract number line scales where children are expected to build up, extend and apply their skills.

Potential challenges

We need to look out for aspects of interpreting and reading scale that some children may find challenging.

Children may fail to realise that, on any given scale, all equal intervals need to be of equal value. Experience of looking at, talking about and exploring a variety of scales can help to consolidate this idea.

Also, if a partial scale line is used (for example, the vertical scale shown in the main part of the lesson, showing 300–400ml), an assumption is sometimes made that the intervals go up in amounts of the first number labelled (in the example referred to, this would be 300ml).

Children might find it difficult to articulate the process. If children are not used to describing/explaining/justifying their thinking, they may not be confident in expressing their ideas. Try to make sure that time is given for children to discuss and rehearse before asking them to share with a larger group; sometimes this gives them the opportunity to try out their ideas and language. Also, make sure that children know you are interested in what they say and sometimes refer to an interesting discussion you may have heard, or maybe one where there was disagreement. Try not to provide what you think is the 'correct solution' or right way of doing something but encourage others to think about and contribute to the debate. Positively acknowledge contributions children make, whether oral or written, but try not to praise where praise is not due. Comments such as, 'Oh, you've really made us think there' or 'I wonder what everyone else thinks' can be made to ensure children keep on thinking, rather than children relying on you to provide an answer/agreement or otherwise.

Ways the lesson could be adapted

Instead of the teacher modelling the process, children could be shown the first scale and asked to discuss, with partners, how they might go about working out other numbers on the marked scale. These ideas can be collected, refined as appropriate and used for further scales.

When working on scales, 'new' numbers or amounts could be given to the children and they could be asked to position them appropriately, giving justification for their decisions.

All the activities could be within the context of measuring scales, using a variety of instruments. The different scales could be explored and questions could be asked about different scales being used for the same aspect of measure.

How the learning might be developed in future lessons

Following on from this lesson, some children will be ready to interpret number lines which extend into negative numbers, fractions and decimals. Ask children to consider if the same way of interpreting the scale can be used and if so, how. Encourage the children to try some out and see what happens. Some children could be challenged further by being asked to design their own scaled number lines, label some points but challenge their peers to work out others. Giving children squared paper saves time when constructing their number lines and does not lessen the demand of the activity.

In future lessons you could ask children to use measuring equipment (measuring cylinders and weighing scales, for example) to explore the intervals used and interpret the scale. Children could be asked to place objects on a weighing instrument and then use the scale to work out how much the objects weigh. Similarly, children could be asked to pour liquid into measuring cylinders and then use the scale to work out how much liquid is in the container.

Graphs and charts, where scale is used along one or more axes, can be explored to find out what scale has been used and then the scales used to determine given points on the graph.

The equivalence between units of measure can be brought into scale-reading activities. Some of the measuring instruments may have more than one unit used on the scale. For example, a measuring cylinder may have millilitres and litres marked along the side of the container. So measurement can be given as millilitres, litres or a combination. Some children will need to spend time making sense of these equivalences but by doing so they will be making sense of numbers and measures. Real-life situations can provide meaningful and relevant contexts.

Key self-evaluation questions to help reflection on practice

- Do I regularly model my thinking to the children? Do I ask children to model their thinking?

- Do I use recording to help model my thinking and the mathematics?

- Do I give the chance for children to rehearse their thinking?

- If I ask children to discuss, do I make it clear what their discussion is about and what they are trying to achieve?

- Do I plan a range of probing questions I can ask during mathematics lessons to help me to assess the depth of children's understanding?

- Do I develop children's understanding of number by encouraging them to visualise numbers in their heads?

Further reading

Interactive teaching program 'Measuring Scales' and guidance notes can be downloaded from **www. teachfind.com/national-strategies/mathematics-itp-measuring-scales**

References

DfE (2013) *The National Curriculum in England Key Stages 1 and 2 Framework Document.* London: Department for Education.

Chapter 13

Moving on

Learning outcomes

This chapter will help you to:

- consider ways in which to develop your practice;
- be aware of how the environment can support children's learning in mathematics;
- think about cross-curricular approaches to teaching and learning in mathematics.

Adapting and building on lessons

All the lesson examples in this book provide suggestions as to how the lessons might be adapted. No 'pre-prepared' lesson plans will fully suit the needs of all of your children or provide you with everything you need to take into account when finalising you plans. However, the approaches and variety in types of activities offer a good range and we suggest you look carefully at these when thinking how you might adapt the lessons.

When you have taught a lesson, you will need to consider to what extent the learning objectives have been met and what the next steps might be. On many occasions, the objectives will need to be revisited; the lesson examples provided are not intended to be used as the sole lesson to achieve an intended learning outcome. In future lessons you might offer children different contexts for their learning or offer different types of activity addressing the same learning. Over time, you will be able to identify aspects that need further learning opportunities or have caused difficulty. Don't be afraid to go back to a stage where children have understood and demonstrated a good grasp of a mathematical idea. If you go forward before children are ready to move on, it is likely that any future learning is superficial and gaps will begin to appear.

There are many features of the lesson examples in this book which can be used when planning all mathematics lessons. These are some to take particular note of:

- different ways in which children are expected to work;

- the balance of types of questions;

- use of models and images;

- how children are encouraged to use mathematical language;

- variety in the nature of the activities;

- ways in which each part of the lesson focuses on learning;

- teacher modelling;

- ways in which children are encouraged to produce their own ideas;

- how the teacher manages feedback and confirms learning.

Reflecting on your own teaching

In the lesson examples provided, there are key self-evaluation questions to help you reflect on your practice. The ability to *reflect systematically on the effectiveness of lessons and approaches to teaching* (DfE, 2012: Standard 4D) is key to improving practice. When you are evaluating a mathematics lesson you have taught you will need to consider a variety of factors. Try to avoid focusing on whether or not children completed the tasks set but look for the quality of children's learning as well as your role in the lesson.

Here are some questions to help you reflect. The list is not exhaustive but helps to focus on important aspects. The extended questions *in italics* are provided to help you to evaluate further.

Did the children:

- understand the objectives? *How do you know?*

- have an opportunity to use their mathematical knowledge, skills and understanding? *What mathematical knowledge, skills and understanding were they using?*

- have the opportunity to explore mathematics? *When were they doing this?*

- have access to images and/or practical resources to support their thinking? *Which resources? When? How were they being used to support thinking?*

- use the appropriate mathematical vocabulary? *Which vocabulary were the children using?*

- give reasons for their answers?

- meet the objective(s)? *How do you know?*

Did you:

- build on knowledge the children already had? *What knowledge were you building on?*

- expose and discuss common mistakes and misconceptions? *What were they?*

- use questioning to extend children's learning? *Were there any specific questions that you thought were effective?*

- model your thinking and ways of working? *When did you do this?*

- create connections between different aspects of mathematics? *Which aspects?*

- encourage paired talk/working? *Was this effective? Why/why not?*

- deploy additional adults effectively?

- review progress children have made? *How did you do this?*

As well as providing some prompts for reflection, these can also be used when you are planning lessons. They might help you to think about whether/how you have incorporated these features and opportunities into your lesson plans.

Learning environment

The learning environment for mathematics can be seen as a resource for learning (Turner, 2013) in various ways. In your classroom, try to make sure there are number lines and grids which reflect the types of numbers the children are working with and make use of them during lessons. You can set up 'working walls' which can serve different purposes. These remain on the classroom wall whilst the ideas on them are appropriate to current learning. So, for example, if you are working on partitioning multi-digit numbers, you may have something similar to Figure 13.1.

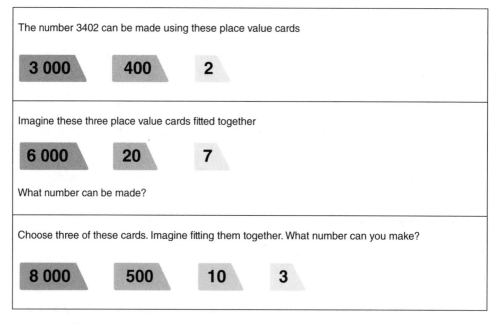

Figure 13.1 Place value cards

The learning environment can go beyond the classroom. Around the school building, numbers are used in different ways. You may ask children to set out as number detectives to search out different uses of number or to locate specific numbers or numbers within given intervals, for example. The main entrance might provide recent attendance figures or termly house points which might be collected and put in order. Encourage children to notice numbers and recognise their significance.

Outdoor areas provide further opportunities. There are lots of reasons for counting. For example, how many children can sit at the outdoor table? There are four of us who want to ride a trike; are there enough trikes? Can we estimate how many children are on the playground? How might we check whether our estimate is close?

Some of the lesson examples suggest using outside space for mathematical activity. Although going outside does not necessarily support mathematics (Turner, 2013), in the examples given, it means that children can spread out and have space to move around or organise themselves. Some playgrounds have number snakes or number grids and these can be ideal for children finding and standing on numbers according to a given rule or instruction, e.g. Can you stand on a number that is less than 25?

Beyond the school site offers further opportunities. In relation to number and place value we might identify extended use of numbers – bus numbers, house numbers, venue seat-numbering system, shop pricing, road numbers and lots more.

But do not forget the learning environment in the sense of ethos and culture of your classroom. You will want to create a classroom which welcomes children's ideas and where children are not afraid to try things out. Try to create a positive learning environment, where the classroom culture is one which welcomes challenge as an opportunity for children to learn (Hansen, 2011).

Here are some points to consider when establishing your classroom culture for positive learning in mathematics:

- When you have asked a question, 'buy time' by saying something such as, 'I'll come back to you for an answer to that question in two minutes' (and do go back). Encourage children to see silence as thinking time (DCSF, 2009).

- Ask children to talk in pairs and make clear what you are expecting them to talk about. Make sure your children know that talking is learning and working.

- Value your children's responses and let them know that you value their thinking, not simply the answer. However, be careful not to overpraise.

- Acknowledge that sometimes children's responses give us all a challenge to think about.

- Try not to play the 'guess what's in my head' game. Be open to various responses and select ones you might want to build on. At times, acknowledge a variety of answers and then ask the children how we are going to decide which one, if any, is the correct answer. Don't feel you always have to be the provider of a 'correct answer'.

- Be prepared to be surprised! Children sometimes give us explanations that we had not thought of. Do not be dismissive but ask further questions if need be and acknowledge that the response has made us think.

- Children seldom give a 'wrong' answer on purpose. Use incorrect answers as learning opportunities and make sure your children know that is what you think, in order to encourage them to feel the same.

- Make sure that responses from children are organised in a way that avoids dominance by particular children.

- You are a key part of the learning community in your classroom; try to think of ways of exhibiting this.

- Try to set up activities where everyone can make a contribution/be involved.

- All children should be challenged; challenge is not just for your high-attaining group!

- Give the opportunity for children to make decisions.

- In review time (plenaries, mini-plenaries) ask the children to say what they are learning; what is difficult and why; what is easy and why.

- Give feedback to children on what they are good at and not so good at and why.

- Provide opportunities for children to ask one another questions.

- Provide opportunities for children to carry out extended tasks to build resilience.

- Give children time to tackle a problem and find ways of overcoming difficulties before you intervene.

- Plan and use additional adult support in varying ways and for varying groups of children.

Cross-curricular learning

Mathematics is a subject that can be applied and mathematical skills can support learning across the curriculum (Haylock, 2010, p14). This means that we should be taking the opportunity for children to realise that their mathematical skills can be used in other curriculum areas and that this adds to the purpose of mathematics. Sometimes I am given comments such as, 'Children didn't even know they were doing mathematics because it was a science lesson', as if this was a good thing. My response is always, 'What a shame!' I think we should make it clear to the children that they are using some of their mathematics skills to support aspects of other curriculum areas.

There are various opportunities to link mathematics with other areas of the curriculum; some are referred to in lesson examples in this book. Haylock (2010) also makes the point that the learning works both ways. Children can use existing mathematics skills and knowledge in other areas of the curriculum and can use the context of another subject area to develop or reinforce mathematical skills and knowledge. Some of the subjects more commonly associated with cross-curricular links are art, music, science, geography, PE, technology and history. For example, numerical data such as distances, temperatures and population figures are just a few aspects that could be used in geography or used to provide context in mathematics lessons.

The best approaches truly integrate learning rather than provide activities at a superficial level. There is nothing wrong with circling the even-numbered birds at a bird table on a worksheet (especially if children have to justify their choice), but let's not pretend this is cross-curricular and relates learning to the topic on playground visitors! Counting the different types of birds that are seen at the bird table at different times of the day, putting the numbers in order and thinking about why the numbers are different is far more cross-curricular.

Key self-evaluation questions to help reflection on practice

- Am I aware of important features of my lessons that I should reflect on?

- Can I think of some ways to establish a positive learning environment?

- Do I know how I might make use of cross-curricular opportunities for children's learning?

References

DCSF (2009) *Moving on in Mathematics*. Nottingham: DCSF Publications.

DfE (2012) *Teachers' Standards*. London: Department for Education.

Hansen, A. (2011) *Children's Errors in Mathematics*. London: SAGE.

Haylock, D. (2010) *Mathematics Explained for Primary Teachers*. London: SAGE.

Turner, S. (2013) *Teaching Primary Mathematics*. London: SAGE.

Glossary of terms

Array   a set of objects or images organised into rows and columns

Cardinal aspect of number   where number is used in counting to describe a set of things e.g. 5 children, 3 pencils, 13 879 football supporters

Commutative   an operation is said to be commutative if the order of numbers makes no difference to the outcome, e.g. $3 \times 5 = 5 \times 3$. Addition and multiplication are commutative; subtraction and division are not commutative

Consecutive   consecutive numbers follow in order, are adjacent in a count. So 6, 7, 8 are consecutive numbers and 40, 45, 50 are consecutive multiples of 5

Decimal number   number expressed in base 10. The term is commonly used when referring to numbers which include a decimal point and represent a whole number plus a fraction of a whole number (tenths, hundredths, etc.), e.g. 34.72

Decimal place   refers to the number of digits to the right of the decimal point. So 5.63 has two decimal places

Decimal point   the punctuation mark in a decimal number separating the whole number part from the fractional part, so the decimal point is always positioned between units and tenths

Digits   individual symbols that are used to build up a number system. For our number system the digits used are 0, 1, 2, 3, 4, 5, 6, 7, 8 and 9. The number 75 is a two-digit number

Hundred square   a 10 by 10 square grid which can be numbered 1 to 100

Integer   a whole number that can be positive or negative; 0 is also an integer

Multi-digit number   a number which has more than one digit. The number 75 is a two-digit number and 5603 is a four-digit number; both are multi-digit numbers

Multiples of a given number   the numbers obtained by multiplying the given number by any whole number greater than zero. So multiples of 5 are 5, 10, 15, 20 and so on

Negative number   a number less than zero

Nominal aspect of number   where number is used as a name or to identify something, e.g. the number 7 bus

Number line   a line on which points are numbered

Number sentence   a mathematical sentence involving numbers, e.g. $3 < 9, 5 + 3 = 8$

Number track   a numbered track where spaces are numbered, not points

Numeral   the symbol used to represent a number

Ordinal aspect of number   where number is used to identify order or relative position in a sequence e.g. first, second, third

Partition   to split a number into component/constituent parts. For example, 48 can be partitioned into 40 + 8 or 30 + 18 or 20 + 28 etc.

Place holder   the role of zero in the place value system of numeration. For example, the zero in the number 307 indicates that there are no tens in that place/column

Place value   the value of a digit in a number that is determined by its place or position in the number. For example, in the number 367, the digit 3 represents 300 or 3 hundreds, the digit 6 represent 60 or 6 tens and the 7 represent 7 ones (or units)

Place value cards (or arrow cards)   sets of cards used to represent the various components/constituent parts of a number

Product   the result of multiplying numbers together. For example, $7 \times 5 = 35$, so 35 is the product of 7 and 5

Roman numerals   the letters of the alphabet that the Romans used to record their numerals

Rounding numbers   the process of expressing a number to a required degree of accuracy. So, if 567 was rounded to the nearest ten it would be 570; if it was rounded to the nearest hundred it would be 600; if it was rounded to the nearest thousand it would be 1 000

Models, images and practical resources

Although we would ultimately like children to count and understand number and place value without reference to supporting models, images and resources, these resources initially serve an important role in providing children with a physical representation of mathematics. This makes abstract concepts more concrete. The models, images and resources below do not form an exhaustive list but are those commonly seen in primary classrooms and are mentioned within the chapters of this book.

Number tracks

1	2	3	4	5	6	7	8	9	10	11	12	13	14	15	16	17	18	19	20

Figure 1   Number tracks

Number tracks are frequently used to support counting in the Early Years Foundation Stage. They normally start at 1 and the numbers label each space. When displayed on a wall they should be at child height. They can also be available in the outdoor learning environment (e.g. drawn on to the ground so children can physically move along the number track).

Hundred squares/1–100 number grid

The hundred square is an extension of a number track. When children start to use a hundred square, ensure that they understand that it is a number track that has been rearranged; imagine a 1–100 number track cut up into strips of ten and then rearranged to form a square. The arrangement of the hundred square can be very useful to help children to see the patterns within the numbers 1–100 (see Figure 2).

Number lines

Number lines differ from number tracks because it is the divisions rather than the spaces that are numbered. This means they can include zero, begin at any number and can extend into negative and decimal numbers. They allow the continuous nature of number to be represented as it is possible, theoretically, to include an infinite number

1	2	3	4	5	6	7	8	9	10
11	12	13	14	15	16	17	18	19	20
21	22	23	24	25	26	27	28	29	30
31	32	33	34	35	36	37	38	39	40
41	42	43	44	45	46	47	48	49	50
51	52	53	54	55	56	57	58	59	60
61	62	63	64	65	66	67	68	69	70
71	72	73	74	75	76	77	78	79	80
81	82	83	84	85	86	87	88	89	90
91	92	93	94	95	96	97	98	99	100

Figure 2 Hundred square/1–100 number grid

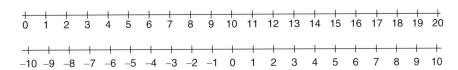

Figure 3 Number lines

of numbers. The number line displayed in a classroom will therefore depend on the range of numbers being explored by the class.

Other examples of number lines could include those in Figure 4. They can be useful when dealing with a large number range and when encouraging children to locate numbers.

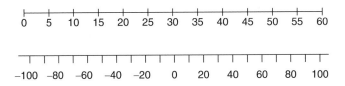

Figure 4 Number lines

Beadstrings

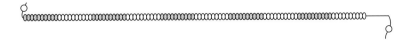

Figure 5 Beadstrings

Beadstrings usually come in lengths of 10, 20 or 100 beads. They provide a representation of numbers that children can physically manipulate. Beadstrings with 100 beads have groups of ten beads in alternate colours. They therefore provide another representation of tens and ones.

Counting sticks

Figure 6   Counting sticks

Counting sticks are usually split into ten equal sections and can be viewed as an unnumbered number line. At a simple level each division can stand for one and so the teacher can use it as a resource to help children count forwards and backwards from 0 to 10. However the counting stick can start at any number and you can count forwards or backwards in steps of any size. It is therefore a flexible resource that can be used throughout the school to support counting in a multitude of different steps and sizes.

Place value cards

Figure 7   Place value cards

Place value cards are also known as arrow cards and can be used to help children construct and partition numbers. They reinforce the language of quantity value as they help children to recognise the 5 in 54 as 50 (see Chapter 5 for more detail).

Place value charts

1 000	2 000	3 000	4 000	5 000	6 000	7 000	8 000	9 000
100	200	300	400	500	600	700	800	900
10	20	30	40	50	60	70	80	90
1	2	3	4	5	6	7	8	9
0.1	0.2	0.3	0.4	0.5	0.6	0.7	0.8	0.9
0.01	0.02	0.03	0.04	0.05	0.06	0.07	0.08	0.09

Figure 8   Place value charts

Place value charts are also known as Gattegno charts after the mathematician Caleb Gattegno. They can help children see how components of numbers can be combined and how this links to how we say numbers. Relevant rows can be displayed and extended as children progress through the primary age phase. For example in Year 1 children may only use the one and tens rows whilst the rows to three decimal places might be displayed in upper Key Stage 2 classrooms.

Place value apparatus

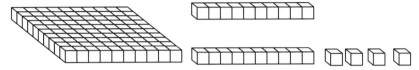

Figure 9 Place value apparatus

Place value apparatus enables children to engage with physical apparatus in order to explore place value in a very concrete way. These are also known as base ten apparatus and Dienes' blocks after the mathematician Zoltan Dienes. The smallest cubes are often referred to as units, the blocks of tens as longs and the blocks of 100 as flats. They can help children appreciate how ten of one type of block can fit together to make one of another block (e.g. ten of the tens blocks fit together to make one of the 100 blocks).

Multiplication grids

Multiplication grids can be used to support children when learning multiplication facts and to identify patterns in multiples. It is important that children understand how the numbers have been generated before they are encouraged to use them.

	1	2	3	4	5	6	7	8	9	10
1	1	2	3	4	5	6	7	8	9	10
2	2	4	6	8	10	12	14	16	18	20
3	3	6	9	12	15	18	21	24	27	30
4	4	8	12	16	20	24	28	32	36	40
5	5	10	15	20	25	30	35	40	45	50
6	6	12	18	24	30	36	42	48	56	60
7	7	14	21	28	35	42	49	56	63	70
8	8	16	24	32	40	48	56	64	72	80
9	9	18	27	36	45	54	63	72	81	90
10	10	20	30	40	50	60	70	80	90	100

Figure 10 Multiplication grid

Index

<, > signs 15, 53–4
   see also Year 2: using < > and = signs – lesson plan
= sign 15, 53–4, 61–2

abacus 101–2
abstraction principle 14
activities 124, 125, 128
   calculator activities 101
   counting activities 14, 18
   extension activities 27, 31
   see also games; rhymes and songs
adapting and building on lessons 124–5
addition 18, 34, 41
adults, role of in class 11, 27, 31, 128
Anghileri, J. 17
answers 27, 109, 121, 127–8
Askew, M. et al. 4, 6, 7, 90
assessment 28, 32

beadstrings 51, 133–4
beliefs about maths teaching 6
big numbers 20, 24, 93–4
   see also Year 5: big numbers – lesson plan
Bird, R. 65
Bloom, B.S. 28
boundary crossings 16
Buchanan, M. 70

calculator activities 101
cardinal aspect of number 13, 14, **130**
classroom ethos and culture 127
Cockburn, A. 6, 33
Cockcroft, W. 13
coins 51, 61
collaboration 91
column value 44
commutative operations 71, **130**
comparison 54
conceptual understanding 5–7
conclusion to lesson 31
confidence 4–5, 11, 24
connections 6–7, 16, 26, 42, 65
consecutive numbers 75, **130**
Council for Learning Outside the Classroom 49
counting 13–14, 15–16, 26
   in multiples 15, 17–18, 19, 22, 23, 64–5
   negative numbers 19
   one more than, one less than 33–5
counting sticks 23, 134
cross-curricular learning 14, 26, 49, 74,
   128–9

decimal numbers 21–2, 104–5, **130**
   see also Year 6: understanding decimals – lesson plan
decimal place 104–5, 110–11, **130**
decimal point 105, 107, **130**
Dienes' blocks 135
differentiation 27, 31, 124
digit cards 100, 102
digit wheel 68
digits 44, **130**
discovery teaching 6
discussion 7–8, 9, 11, 70, 80, 90, 109, 121

equal to (= sign) 15, 53–4, 61–2
errors 29, 90
extension activities 27, 31

feedback 7, 31, 90, 125, 128
fewer than 34
flashcards 71
fluency in mathematics 5
focused learning objectives 10, 26, 29, 124, 125
four-digit numbers 20
fractions 21, 105

Gallistel, C.R. 13–14
games 79–80
   Bingo 81
   Capture Three 77–8, 80
   Higher or Lower 81–2
   matching games 71
   Place Invaders 101
   place value 101, 102
Gattegno charts *see* place value charts
Gelman, R. 14
generalisation 109, 114
Gifford, S. 40
glossary of terms **130–1**
good *vs.* satisfactory maths teaching 9, 10–11
graphs and charts *see* scales; Year 6: reading scales – lesson
   plan
group work 10–11, 90

Hansen, I. 90
Haylock, D. 4, 5, 6, 8, 33, 65, 109, 128
Hindu–Arabic numeral system 43, 85
hundred squares 18, 34, 71, 91, **130**, 132, 133

independence 9, 11
individual work 10–11, 30
instrumental understanding 5
integers **130**